PLANET DANCING

Patrick McCusker

The desire to protect species from extinction must move beyond the commitment of the few. It must move beyond the hope of conserving Indian rhino or the great whales or Japanese crested ibis. It needs to move beyond concerns for rainforests. It needs to move to a position to win the minds of people towards an accomodation of nature on this planet.

There appears to be a widespread *wish* that things might be different. A wish, however, is not enough. A wish is not the same as a *want*. The difference is one of degree of emotion. And whether a species survives or not hangs on that distinction.

Planet Dancing is an attempt to show us the magnificence of nature, even in the small, and to entice us to embrace a number of unusual conservation ideas in which we can all play a part.

PLANET DANCING

Patrick McCusker

OPEN GATE PRESS
incorporating Centaur Press
LONDON

First published in 2011 by Open Gate Press,
51 Achilles Road, London NW6 1DZ

Copyright © 2011 by Patrick McCusker
All rights, by all media, reserved.

British Library Cataloguing-in-Publication Programme
A catalogue record for this book is available from the British Library.

ISBN 978-1-871871-70-8

Illustrations by Paul Francis

Cover design by Frank O'Reilly

The quotation on the front cover is
attributed to J. W. v. Goethe

e-mail address of author: planctdancing@gmail.com
blog address: patmccusker.wordpress.com

Printed and bound in Great Britain by Imprint Digital, Exeter, Devon

Contents

List of Illustrations   vii
Dedication   viii

PART 1

The unstoppable rhythm of the piano	11
Sharing the happiness of frogs (Ontario, Canada)	12
Stop the piano and hear the music	15
Tapestry	16
The Indian canoe and the alligator (Florida, USA)	17
Whirligigs	21
Jellyfish east of Malindi (Kenya)	23
The heron coming down (Ireland)	28
A home for children (Australia)	29
Ancient eyes in the surf (Gulf of Mexico)	34
A short existence (British Columbia, Canada)	36
Word-dancing without music in Norway	38
Three cheers for the little guy (Banff National Park, Canada)	41
There's big – and then there's big! (Seychelles Islands)	43
The 9000km egg (Southern Africa)	44
The big guy in an English swamp	49
In wilderness is the way (Ontario, Canada)	52
Jamaica drift (Jamaica and Scotland)	56
Salamander	59
Tiger day (India)	60
Echoes in the sea	70
Silence in Madagascar	72

PART 2

Meeting again with old friends	77
No guilt	79
Are all species 'useful'?	87
The loss of the familiar	91
The adventure of existence itself	97

SIX CONSERVATION PROPOSALS

1. **The Giving of Nature Names**   103
   (Remembering Encounters with Nature)

2. **The Children-of-the-World Nature Reserve**   114
   (A World Event for Nature)

3. **The Quest Through Togetherness**   121
   (The Creation of a World Wilderness Reserve by the Great Religions of the World)

4. **I will kill the last parrot on Earth**   128
   (On Poverty and the Protection of Species)

5. **The Hundred-Million-Dollar Club**   140
   (Business and Nature)

6. **Dance, Children, for all that is Music!**   146
   (A World Dance Day for Nature)

The land of the Bisnois (India)	148
Dream of a world you would like (Résumé)	150
Addendum: Poets dreaming	159

List of Illustrations

Two islands	viii
The scientist as priest	10
Old man and small boy looking into mist	14
Canoe in a Florida swamp	20
Two jellyfish	22
Daddy with two children in a eucalyptus forest	31
Two horseshoe crabs	35
Delegates with sherry glasses	39
Sooty tern landing on a coco de mer seed	42
Boy finding entada bean in the sea	57
Salamander with beetle on rock	59
Tail flukes of a great whale sticking out of the water	71
Sketch of the island of Madagascar	73
Snail with three leaves	76
Mouse swinging in the corn	85
Park ranger with fox cub and two boys	120
Mountain view (Wilderness reserve)	125
African huts	139
Children dancing in a circle	147

For

Olive, Cliona, Gillian and Philip
who dance under the sun.

All knowledge is not taught in one school.
Hawaiian saying

PART I

The unstoppable rhythm of the piano

Many who would conserve the world on our behalf offer us statistics. They instruct us that we are destroying the forests. They tell us that we are killing the seas; that we are poisoning the air. They chant reasons at us for all of these problems. The mantras become a drumming in our brains. Then we go deaf. There is a sense of unease about. We are no longer sure. No longer are we comfortable either with ourselves or with our world. The drift away from the stabilizing influence of religion – of any sort – is part of the difficulty. Also, there is the fundamental problem of modern man not being able to fully comprehend the world in which he lives.

Most people no longer understand most things. It's not that we don't know the nature of quarks or genotoxins or the morphodynamic behaviour of beaches. We don't even know what's in the processed foods we eat. We have difficulty distinguishing between the synthetic and the real. We have traded understanding for comfort. We have traded dignity in the process.

Around the late 1940s we reached out as never before to science. Science would solve all problems. It would give us comforts beyond the dreams of kings.

And indeed science did produce fabulous and strange wonders. Many of these wonderful things poisoned our water, poisoned our air and damaged our ozone. They seeped into ancient buildings and rotted the stones. They choked the breath out of deep lakes. They trickled into our food, into our lungs, into our brains and into our very DNA. We are uneasy.

It is strange that intelligence has given us these things.

Sharing the happiness of frogs
Ontario, Canada

I clapped my hands and the chorus went silent. Not a sound. A full minute passed – then off to my right a single exploratory croak. Others then, and more still – until the narrow swamp was alive once more with the sound of frogs. There may have been frogs, many frogs, but none were visible. The surface of the swamp was a uniform green lid. But where was the choir? Not a frog could I see. Yet clearly frogs were there, there in abundance, close, loud and insistent. Again I clapped my hands. Total silence. Then that single reflective croak once more – and the slow build-up to a cacophony of song that said it was great to be a frog in an Ontario swamp. That said too: 'Hey man, we've a right to be frogs. We've a right to make frog songs and shout our joy at existence.'

I looked carefully at the swamp once more. Not a croaker was visible. A mat of floating vegetation stretched away in all directions. I was determined to see frogs, to see them in their wonderful din of exuberance and in their simple joy of being frogs.

I then did something that to most people who have not been in wild places would seem unusual. I slipped quietly, fully clothed, into the swamp until I stood neck-deep with swamp weeds brushing my chin.

Now, from every direction about me – the sound of frogs. Big boomers and the endless repeated chirp and trill of lesser weights. Then I saw them. By laying the side of my face against the mat of swamp weeds I could run my eye out along the surface of the swamp. Hundreds of frogs, thousands of frogs, stretching away into the distance. Each face protruded at the same angle out of the swamp. All were turned in the direction of the bank. All the backs were submerged. Only the faces dimpled the surface of the swamp. The green web of weeds concealed each face and head.

From the bank, looking down, everything had been uniformly green – and frog-invisible. Only by being in the water and scanning an eye along the plane of the surface was it possible to see the hummocks of faces sticking out above the surface of the swamp.

I clapped my hands once more and the lid of the swamp clamped closed. Not a frog to be seen. When the chorus again returned I clapped my hands as before. Once more complete silence. We, the frogs and I, played our game many more times. Then I climbed out of the water and went on my way, my clothes drying in the heat of the Canadian sun. Behind me I heard a single tentative croak. Then others, and still more. Slowly the drum of frog-noise drew away as I moved further from the swamp, until I was left with the surf-like sound of wind in the pines above my head.

But on that day I had had an adventure with frogs that has stayed with me down the years.

Stop the piano and hear the music

Perhaps we will never know reality through science alone. A biologist may throw out a line and draw in a very small fish – but he cannot pull in the water in which the fish swims. Science can tell us something of fatty acids. It can tell us of zygotes and polar bodies but it cannot give us an understanding of 'whale' or of the 'silence of butterflies'. It cannot talk to us of the 'comprehension of ghost fish'. It cannot tell us of the 'sadness or happiness of kelp flies'. Perhaps most things will never be knowable through science. Perhaps most things will never be knowable at all. Yet we are uncomfortable with this. We are uncomfortable unless we forge out some sort of reality. What reality do we give to nature? We seem to want to first de-spiritualise it. That way we get rid of the mystery. Then we can begin to see objects – without connections. With that in place each thing suddenly becomes vulnerable. A small step then to demean it and to place it under the label of 'resource'. Now it can be exploited.

The Hawaiian people have a word – *Lokahi*. They use this word to define *Unity-Nature-God*. *Lokahi* should be the conservation word of this new century.

Tapestry

Should we not shed our concern about extinctions? From the time of the green algae all species have fought for dominance. All are locked together – the winner taking all in the Olympic Games of the Genes. If what we do is no more than a process of nature, why hide it? Should we not shout out our success? Why don't we stand up and roar our triumph into the faces of clouded leopards?

The Indian canoe and the alligator
Florida, USA

Nothing surpasses an Indian canoe. It will float in a few inches of water. A touch of a paddle has it on the move. It can be extraordinarily silent, a dribble of water from a reaching paddle the only sound. Slipping among reeds a man in a canoe can approach the stilt-walking poetry of gallinules. Catfish, the granddaddy-faces in the mud, will barely nudge aside for the passage of a canoe.

In a Florida swamp an alligator turned like a compass needle. It pointed its barely-above-water eyes at the bow of a canoe. The canoe glided between the flooded trunks of cypress trees and into the lemon water of the main channel. The alligator was not a "big 'un" as alligators go, but it was big enough for a boy to tell his dad – "Saw a huge 'gator today, pop." Size did not bother the alligator. He did not know what size meant. He knew strength. He respected strength. Twice he had been defeated by the strength of the green alligator with the one eye. Yes, he respected strength, but he never made a linkage between size and strength. You simply went at it as best you could, and if it came back at you worse than you could give – then you backed off.

The alligator eyed the canoe again. Not that he would attack a canoe. Canoes were not creatures of the swamp. Viewed from low down in the water the head of the man sitting in the stern appeared to brush against the canopy of trees that arched across the channel. The canoe drew nearer. The alligator stared at it with indifference. Come the evening he would not be indifferent. He would go cunning and slip along the mud bank in pursuit of young egrets. But for now he was content to laze in the slow drift of the swamp and idly watch the passage of the canoe. He was content to dream of another battle with the green alligator. He did not know why he wanted to fight old One Eye – but he knew that he must. One day young 'gators of his own would explode among the mud hens – but first he had to defeat One Eye. The canoe pushed nearer. It pushed a passage through a raft of soft swamp weeds. Water reflected from the side of the canoe. The paddle barely dimpled the silk surface of the swamp. It left dime-sized whirlpools each time it cleared the water. Sidestepping a knuckle of swamp cypress the canoe slipped past the water creature. The man turned his head towards the alligator. He saw the tell-tale snout pressed low down in the water and lifted his paddle in acknowledgement.

"Hi ya, big fella."

He did not turn the canoe in the direction of the 'gator nor did he increase his forward pace. On a slow drift the alligator stared at the receding canoe. He stared out of expressionless eyes until the canoe disappeared from view among the drowned cypress trees.

Then the alligator went back to his dream state. Again he thought of old One Eye. He would take him next time round. In a great lethargy of contentment in the assurance of the outcome with One Eye, the alligator drifted in the slow current that moved in the swamp. Broadside on, he nudged over a mud bank barely awash with yellow water. The tips of the alligator's claws scored across the soft surface of the fluid mud beneath him. The swamp deepened once more. His claws dragged clear of the bank and again hung limply down into the tepid water. For a long time the alligator drifted. He did not know time. He knew shadows. When the shadows were long he would skirt the mud banks and slip under the keels of pintails.

A splash. The alligator turned in a slow arc. A canoe knifed into view. It moved with authority. A fat man, wearing a wide-brimmed hat, sat in the stern. Moving his head from side to side in an impatient way, the man flashed his eyes among the flying buttresses of the drowned cypress trees. Under the weight of the man and the forward thrust of the canoe the bow was lifted clear of the swamp. The alligator's snout barely dimpled the surface of the water. Eyes, half-drowned, watched the approaching canoe. The man saw the tell-tale eyes. He slipped the paddle out of the yellow of the water. Under its own momentum the canoe continued to cut forward. The eyes of the man never once left the ancient eyes in the swamp, eyes that would soon be among pintails when the shadows grew long. The alligator hung in the water. Then the first of the tiny bow waves running out before the canoe touched against the snout of the animal and rippled along its body. An explosion. The alligator's world exploded into pain and noise and disorientation. The first bullet tore through one of his eyes, the second slammed into the soft tissue of his throat. A steel hook on a hank of rope flashed over the side of the canoe. It caught and then ruptured the flesh under the alligator's jaw. The curved spike would prevent the prize from sinking. Swirling the canoe around, the man brought it tight against the dead alligator.

Later that evening in a Florida swamp, when the shadows lay long on the mud banks, when old One Eye had become cautious, when the ibis were safe at roost, two canoes approached each other down the long channel. In the back of one sat a tall man, his paddle dipping and rising at a slow, judged pace. The fat man sat in the stern of the second canoe. His paddle did not display as fine a cut. The men drew nearer.

"Howdy. A fine evening." The tall man lifted his arm in acknowledgement of the other canoeist. "How there." The fat man touched stubby fingers against the side of his hat.

In the quiet of a Florida evening, in the quiet of a Florida swamp, the canoes drew nearer. Each man used his paddle as a break. Each was eager to talk of what he had seen in the swamp. The canoes drew alongside. The space of a foot of water separated them. "Got a good 'un back along," the man with the wide-brimmed hat said. He nodded towards the bottom of his canoe.

The tall man looked into the canoe. A raw alligator skin lay in a mush over a coil of rope. After a moment he lifted his head and stared into the half-concealed face under the wide-brimmed hat:

"Why d'you shoot 'im?" he said.

The fat man shrugged his shoulders: "Fifteen dollars a square foot for belly skin."

The canoes lay side by side a moment without touching. Around them the long shadows darkened. A one-eyed alligator, well concealed under a branch of a fallen tree, looked at the canoes out of his good eye. Without a sound the snout and head submerged under the water. The men sitting in their canoes looked along the channel in opposite directions. Neither spoke further. There was no longer a place for words. Each man knew that. Each held to his view of what it was to be in a Florida swamp. Both men, neither one before the other, both together touched their paddles into the lemon water. The canoes drew apart and moved away from each other down the long channel – until each was lost from view.

Whirligigs

What a strange name. And there they are dancing across the surface of the pond. They had been there yesterday, and there the day before, all dancing with consummate exuberance. These small beetles are the dervish dancers of the meniscus layer.

Whirligigs – only the things themselves, only their madcap dancing could force us to invent such a name. Without whirligigs it would be inconceivable to imagine that such spinning creatures could exist at all. Yet they do. God, what were you thinking the day you invented these strange little beings? You must have laughed and delighted in what you had created. And when you placed them on their first pond how they must have spun and danced for you. You must have known back then that when we too came along, we would also delight in seeing these spinning tops out on the water. And in their magnificent whirr they throw the question back into our faces – why should there be whirligigs at all?

Jellyfish east of Malindi
Kenya

Twenty kilometres out from Malindi, on the Kenyan coast, a water creature drifted in the immensity of the great Indian Ocean. It had drifted for days. It was what marine scientists like to call a coelenterate or a member of the Phylum Cnidaria – as though a name gave some sort of understanding about the thing itself. This strange name was not known by any of the sea creatures that lived in all of that ocean. None of them had names. They existed without names, without classification – and had done so long before the classifiers had announced that naming things was important.

The great jellyfish drifted in the warm Somali Current. It was mid-August. In the water around her there were thousands of others, all in the great drift northwards, in the silence of the ocean. Once she had been but a speck of life. Then she had grown into something strange, something strange to human eyes but not to a jellyfish: she had become a tiny flat thing cloaked in a fringe of hairs. Biologists labelled this development in the life of a jellyfish the planula larva stage. For days, protected by nothing more than her insignificance, this flat creature searched for something, not knowing what she was looking for. Finally a black tower of rock blocked her way. The larva floated up the side of the rock and came to rest on a sloping ledge. What had been a flat larva now became a gelatinous rod. The rod became a stack of tiny buttons, one above the other. The buttons matured, and floated free – each a jellyfish on the journey towards adulthood. These swimming buttons, these hardly-there-at-all jellyfish, would grow in size and would be called medusae by scientists. Those who were not scientists would call them jellyfish, because they looked like jelly floating in the sea. Whatever they were called or not called, they would grow into big jellyfish.

Jellyfish live in a world of the senses. A change in salt concentration registers. A drop in oxygen is noted. Temperature is important. When the temperature edges up jellyfish descend to a lower depth, until their sensory world is again in balance. These qualities of sea water are important to all jellyfish.

In her silent world the great jelly creature trailed her net of stinging threads. She had been trawling for days without success. Then one of her threads triggered a surge of poison. A tiny fish shuddered. A second, then a third thread struck out at the fish. Poison exploded through the prey. In that fashion did the jellyfish make a simple living. Then she pulsed onwards again through the warm water. Her journey was carrying her to a reef bed. There she would release prodigious numbers of eggs to dance in the sperm clouds of others. Few eggs would survive to become planula larvae, fewer still to become stationary polyps. And very few indeed would become full-grown medusae. But there would be a few – as there had been for millions of years.

In the green water, near the shoreline of Malindi, two fishermen on a small dhow drifted on the swell of that great ocean. The little craft moved in harmony with the rhythm of the sea. The men spoke of the love for a woman. They were Kenyans of the Bajun people and came from the town of Malindi. They spoke in Swahili:

Yeye ni mwangaza wa maisha yangu ['She is the light of my life'], the taller of the two men said. He sat at the tiller of the little boat. *Atakuwa mke wangu siku moja* ['She will be my wife one day'].

"You will need to catch many fish, Mahammed Suleiman. Amina is beautiful, so her family will expect riches."

"I will catch fish. I will pull so many blues out of the sea that her father will greet me with respect beyond my years," Mahammed said gravely. He brought the tiller around. "Perhaps we will catch a suli." The wind coming off Malindi Point puffed full the saffron sail. The tiny boat nodded over the swell and moved further out from the coast to where the yellowfins ran.

Mahammed glanced at his friend Bakari sprawled out on the net. He knew his friend was right. Amina would want him to be a warrior. She would want him to be a provider. She would expect that, because her father, and her family, would expect that. Mahammed Suleiman leaned over the side of the boat to see beyond the reach of the saffron sail. The Indian Ocean lay empty to the horizon. It was empty even of the ugly cargo boats that hugged the coast carrying sisal and pineapples out of Mombasa to Mogadishu and beyond.

The great jellyfish sensed the first thin vibrations running through the water. The pressure wave was hardly discernable. Sensory cells, however, registered change. Vibrations increased, became small wavelets, then stopped. The ocean was as before – only darker. Above the jellyfish the keel of Mahammed's boat, with its necklace of barnacles, rises and falls with the swell. For a moment the small boat hung in the water without moving. Then something flashed briefly on the surface of the sea. A great sinking all around; the vortex of the dropping net swept the jellyfish sideways and into the nylon mesh. The net continued to sink. It sank down to where the yellowfins ran. Again and again the jellyfish struck out against the encircling net. The net stopped its descent. It hung like a gaping, wide-mouthed creature in the immensity of the sea. It hung without movement.

A small skipjack struck the net; then three falusi struck, their gills locked. The net continued to hang without moving. Time passed. The jellyfish had no sensation of time. She registered the cut of nylon string against her side. The strands of net held her hopelessly entangled. Time passed. Without warning two yellowfins flashed through the water and exploded simultaneously into the net. The impact reverberated along the strands of nylon, slicing through three of the tentacles of the jellyfish. The severed threads rippled free of the net; curling and uncurling, they slipped into the deep waters below.

In the dhow the impact of the big fish ran in the rope wrapped around the hardened knuckles of Mahammed Suleiman. He sprang to his feet shouting. Together the two men took the strain and steadily drew the net up out of the depths. The yellowfins fought the net, and with each thrash of their great tails the nylon cut deeper into the side of the jellyfish. Hand over fist, at a practised pace, the men pulled at the ropes and dragged the fish upward. The net rose glistening out of the warm sea. Muscle, sinew, the beating of men's hearts and the love of one man for his woman worked the heavy net over the side of the boat. The three falusi, flaming with colour, were the first to be wrenched free. They lay together gasping, wide-eyed, the fog of blanketing net thickening over them. One of the yellowfins, still full of fight, thrashed its heavy body, and falling into the boat shuddered on top of the falusi. Mahammed killed it with one blow. Then the second yellowfin flashed over the side into the dhow. The jellyfish, hopelessly entangled in the net, slid into the boat. Even now, in spite of her deep lacerations, if placed back into the ocean she would still live to dance her eggs in the sea. The solitary skipjack was dragged aboard. It fell free of the net and fluttered about the feet of Mahammed. Then there was no more net in the sea.

Mahammed and Bakari Abdullah sat hunched, drawing salt air into their heaving lungs. After a few minutes Mahammed worked his toe against the side of the skipjack and picking it up flung it over the side of the boat. "Watch out," Bakari shouted, nodding at the net. Mahammed Suleiman followed his gaze and drew the net towards him. He folded it about his feet until the jellyfish, shimmering like diesel oil, lay on the seat in front of him. Picking up a wooden mallet he repeatedly smashed it down on her. The world of the great jellyfish became an explosion of pain and collapsed into a nightmare of dying. She released her eggs in a desperate hope that some might still dance in the sea. Again and again the wooden mallet struck until the jellyfish was reduced to paste. Then Mahammed lifted the bit of net over the side of the boat and washed it in the ocean until all traces of the jellyfish were gone, until the nylon mesh dripped clean as though the creature had never existed.

Together the fishermen examined the two yellowfins. In turn they held each tuna in their arms and discussed the weight: "Forty kilos." They could agree on that. "The other?" "Sixty, maybe sixty-five." "Sixty-five."

The tuna would go for a good price. The falusi they would keep for supper – they were good to eat. Mahammed Suleiman read the sky. The wind had changed and the first traces of dark clouds stained the horizon. "We're in for a storm," he said. Bakari nodded in agreement.

They were far from the Kenyan shoreline now. Mahammed worked the tiller and turning the boat felt for the best direction to fill the sail. He aimed the bow towards Casuarina Point far ahead in the smouldering blaze of the setting sun, and the little boat ran before the wind towards the safety of home.

The heron coming down
Ireland

A great grey bird came down the dawn sky. It came without hurry. It came out of a very ancient wisdom of what it is to be a heron coming down. Cutting through the silence of the thin morning air, a solitary croak ran before the heron to announce his coming to the reedbed far ahead. The sound too was ancient and unknowable to men.

Slate-bird of the morning, it ghosted over the lake and cut a furrow through the mist that smoked from the surface of the water. The bird dropped lower, its shadow slipping through the mist. Far ahead, the reedbed oozed away from the land and into the water as though in eagerness to welcome home the great bird. Reeds and herons were companions from a long time ago, each incomplete without the other.

Then the *crak-crak* of the heron, crisp as Arctic ice, like the bark of a fox in winter, acknowledged the familiarity of the reedbed. The tips of the reeds bowed willingly under the keel of the great bird. Wings, like skimmed smoke, billowed, banked, braked. The heron danced down through the gilded rise of the reeds and with a deliberate folding of the great wings settled onto the spongy ground below.

In the stillness that lay across the lake that morning I sat in the comfort of a heron nearby.

A home for children
Australia

Australia is an enormous country yet few people live there. In a tall eucalyptus forest of that ancient continent a small bird stood about under a gum tree. It stared at the ground as though what it had found was the answer to everything, as though all its future happiness depended on that spot.

Then the small bird did a strange thing. It took a twig and worked the base of it into the ground, so that the twig stood upright. The bird found another twig and planted it beside the first. Again and again it left the clearing only to return with fresh twigs. Soon it had built two walls of twigs fifteen centimetres apart and almost a metre in length. The tips of the twigs bent inward, so that when viewed from a short distance away the little bird's creation looked like a tiny hut in the forest.

But things were not yet as they should be. From a stream the bird collected yellow bones, the remnants of a dead sheep now hopelessly twisted around a partially submerged rock. One by one the bird placed these treasures in front of the little hut. Then – something better than bones: three red pebbles that lay together on a flush of dry sand above the reaches of the river. The bird picked up the pebbles and placed them carefully among the display of bones. What else might be needed? A dead beetle that glowed with a green hue was cause for excitement. Bits of snail shells, berries, feathers – all of these were added to the bone garden. Then a discovery more valuable than all the others – a splinter of blue glass. This was indeed a find. The bird placed it next to one of the red pebbles. The piece of glass made a big difference.

Satisfied at last, the bird stepped out of the drumming heat into the hut and stared watchfully at his fine creation outside. For a long time he stayed there without moving. Then, with growing anxiety, he repeatedly scanned the canopy of trees above the clearing. The hiss and chirp and whirr of unseen insects filled his head. A sharp scent of eucalyptus oil pervaded the hut. The bird continued to observe carefully his lovely garden display and the branches above.

Then a shadow. It flitted momentarily above the hut and was gone again. The small bird jumped. Running nervously into his fine garden he repeatedly looked into the trees. Again the shadow, now more than a shadow, appeared in the canopy above. Finally the shadow settled onto a branch of a bottlebrush tree. The tiny bird stared at the branch. A beautiful bird was looking back down at him.

The life of the small bowerbird slammed into a frenzy. It was not that he broke out into song, the whole bird became a dance. So wildly did he turn and turn about that it seemed as if his entire life had been but a preparation for this single moment. He danced in his fine garden that displayed a tiny piece of blue glass. To add to the attractiveness of the display he repeatedly picked up one of the red pebbles. He picked up the dead beetle with the green hue and, tipping back his head, held the beetle up towards the bottlebrush tree. Finally, he stood beside the pride of it all, the piece of blue glass. He lifted it in happiness and held it out towards the female.

Once more the shadow flitted in the bottlebrush tree. Then she dropped to the ground and approached the display of twigs. How the little bowerbird danced then. He danced his heart out until he felt that he must simply burst with love. The joy of his life entered the hut. Carefully she examined the structure, scrutinizing the twigs and their positioning. Without let-up the small bird danced in his garden for her. Finally the female stepped out of the hut and examined the garden, and without warning exploded from the ground and

became silhouetted against the sun. Then she was gone. The dance of the little bird collapsed away. He stood in his garden anxiously searching the sky, but the bottlebrush tree remained empty. For a long time the bowerbird stood about in his unhappiness. The heat of the day rolled in waves across the dry forest floor. The bird looked aimlessly at his garden, at the few really fine decorations that were there. More was needed. Resolve grew once again. He would need additional items, decorations that would be exceedingly grand. He needed things to turn a small bird's heart to love.

Four hundred metres from his bower the bird discovered a cache of great wealth – three pieces of blue glass. He sat in a gum tree and stared down at the glass, hardly daring to believe his good fortune. The pieces of glass formed part of a rival bowerbird's display garden. The bower was deserted. He quickly dropped to the ground and snatching up two of the pieces flitted through the forest for home. A second journey pirated away the remaining piece of glass. When placed among the sheep bones the three additions made a fine difference to his garden.

With the new ornamentations in place, the bowerbird once again stepped into his hut. Suddenly a beautiful bowerbird dropped straight down and landed right among the decorations.

Electrified, the small bird scrambled out of his hut in welcome – welcome – welcome. He once more ran off into his little dance display, circling the beautiful bird that had come into his garden. How he stomped his tiny feet. She carefully inspected the garden. Notice the blue glass! Notice the blue glass! She noticed the pieces of glass. She inspected the twig hut as though it said something important about the dancing bird. She disappeared into the mesh of twigs – and emerged again. The male bowerbird's heart soared. His world exploded onto a new plane of love: she had accepted him. Above all the others she had accepted him. How his little feet danced. She had accepted him as a fine bower builder. She accepted him above all the other bower builders in the forest.

Afterwards, the beautiful female bowerbird, as is the nature of bowerbirds, left the male and built a nest in a tree to rear her young.

It was about this time that the Australian Authorities gave permission to a man and a woman to build a house. They decided to build it where the bowerbird's simple display was already located. Earth-moving machines crushed flat the tiny hut and swept away the sheep bones and red pebbles and the tiny pieces of blue glass.

Today, a beautiful house stands where once a fine bowerbird's hut used to be. The children of the house play among the gum trees. Daddy has promised that he will bring them into the forest to see if there are any bowerbirds left in that part of Australia.

Ancient eyes in the surf
Gulf of Mexico

Some years ago I spent a wonderful ten days on an island nature reserve in the Gulf of Mexico. It was the first time that I saw horseshoe crabs. They indeed looked like the shape of horseshoes and their domed backs gave the impression of small turtles coming in out of the surf. Everything about them spoke of 'ancient'. Indeed, they have been around for over three hundred and fifty million years.

But in the world of these horseshoe crabs there is now a problem; they are harvested for a property in their blood. Their blood is strange in that it is copper-based. Scientists utilize this property to test for the presence of bacteria.

In the past, too, there were pressures on horseshoe crabs. Once they could be counted in their millions – and that was a problem; such vast numbers made it economic to harvest them for processing into animal feed and fertilizer.

Horseshoe crabs still come into the shallows of the waters of the Gulf of Mexico – but in far fewer numbers now.

A short existence
British Columbia, Canada

Northwards from the beautiful city of Vancouver, in British Columbia, at a distance that an erratic crow might fly in a number of weeks, a huge river, the Skeena, forms a large pool where salmon lie. Fishermen stand on the banks of this great pool and arc their *Kit-A-Mat* spoons through the air and down to the salmon far below.

Above the fishermen's heads storm clouds move steadily inland. The shadows of the clouds on the great pool increase the prospect of fish. For days the clouds have been on the move. They stack up against the mountains and drop rain. It is the end of April. The rain falls on the deep accumulation of the winter's snow. It is the first unquestionable sign of spring returning to that part of Canada.

What was beautiful and white in winter dulls to a half-brother of rain and sloughs down the mountain in slushy wedges of dying snow. It slips and collapses into little canyons and moves rapidly downward through rivers too small to have names. Finally it thunders into the great roar of the Skeena. The meltwater boils with exuberance and claws and snatches at mud and sand that had been safe when all was frozen. Now all is on the move. Ten feet of snow is on the move. The lead-grey of the sky and the lead-grey of the mountainsides, all is on the move – so much water that the very sides of the river shudder and weaken. Islands of vegetation break free, float, nudge out into the maelstrom of the main flow and are swept downriver. Chocolate-brown, the water is more mud than river.

Fishermen at the pool of fish hurriedly draw in their

lines. An island, with spruce trees and a black bear upon it, sweeps into view and thunders into the great pool. The bear, master of his revolving kingdom, stares at the men on the banks. The island, like a living creature, feels for the tug that will draw it further down the river. Again the current grows stronger. Bear Island, trawling a net of trees in its wake, drains out of the pool of fish. It gathers pace. Bucking and heaving, it sweeps away from the view of the fishermen and swirls off down the great river. The men spin their lures through the air once more.

Millions of tons of mud and sand ride piggyback in the great surge of meltwater. They ride the water all the way to the Pacific Ocean and far out to sea; there they sink, grain after grain, out of the light into the darkness. Each grain finally lies still on the bottom of the sea in the utter silence, where a moose bellow in the Fall will never be heard. And all around in that darkness, a continuous settling down – each sand particle and each silt particle with its own story to tell. Eventually, with the passing of an amount of time beyond understanding, five thousand metres of rock will rise above the surface of the sea.

At such a far time as this, the Skeena River will be without trace, the pool of fish long gone. And in this distant place people, who know about these things, will say: "It took millions of years to lay down this mountain of rock. It is made of sand and mud which great rivers carried to the sea." And somewhere in that sedimentary mountain a favoured person will find the bones of a small bear that walked on the Earth. People, on seeing the newly discovered fossil, will shake their heads and try to imagine what it must have been like when there were bears in the world.

Word-dancing without music in Norway

"John, can I count on your support?" asked the Norwegian.

"What's the issue?" The smaller man looked carefully at the Scandinavian. He looked for signs.

"Oh, it's the same old thing – this proposal on whaling."

"Oh, that!"

"A curtailment is all very well – but in its place, John, in its place."

The smaller man shrugged his shoulders: "Whales aren't in the numbers they used to be. Fewer nowadays," he said.

"Maybe, but there could be more than we think."

"I'm not saying you're wrong, but the scientific papers are beginning to stack the other way."

"Scientists have been wrong before. There's a lot of ocean out there, most of it miles deep. How can anyone know for sure what the numbers really add up to?"

"But suppose this time they're right. What then?"

"I agree, I agree – nobody would want that. That's what we're here for – to agree a sensible arrangement." For a moment the Norwegian delegate said nothing more, content to look thoughtfully at his British counterpart. Then he added:

"Talking of sensible arrangements – how is your drift-net proposal coming on?"

The small man took a glass of sherry from a passing tray:

"Well, I still hold to the view that we can't just ban drift-netting. When you're from a fishing constituency ... well, you know how it is."

The Norwegian nodded: "Indeed I do, indeed I do. How do you think it will go in the end?"

"With the weakening of the fishing lobby now a reality it's hard to call. It could go either way. We're all for conservation, but there has to be a balance."

The Norwegian raised his hand in understanding:

"Who can argue with that? Whether it's whales or driftnets it comes down to the same thing – jobs and home-grown politics."

The men stared at each other. It was all in their eyes.

"Whether we like it or not that's the reality we have to work with," the smaller man said.

The tall man looked carefully: "When people really want us to legislate in a meaningful way for conservation – well, what are politicians for?" He looked again at the other man. "So, on this whaling thing – I can depend on your support?"

The small man looked at his nails: "Well, my government's position on whaling is still fluid. We feel … "

The Norwegian understood: "We need to hunt whales, John, just as you need drift-nets. It's really the same issue. Different meetings, but the issues are the same."

Standing in the hotel lobby, crowded with other delegates waiting to be called for the vote, the two men knew they had reached an understanding. With a slight tinkling sound they touched glasses. The call for the vote on the banning of hunting minke whales rang out across the lobby.

Three cheers for the little guy
Banff National Park, Canada

At first I found it difficult to see them. Then ... there they were! Like tiny garden snails they were rafting together in little groups of a dozen or more. I was down on my knees bending over a sulphur-rich spring in Banff National Park in Canada.

According to the park experts there are only five known populations of these snails in existence. Their needs are simple – feeding on algae and bacteria in the springs.

A really big guy in the world of these snails would be no larger than a pea. But conservation is not just about protecting the big and the conspicuous. Little fellows too should have a place in our thoughts.

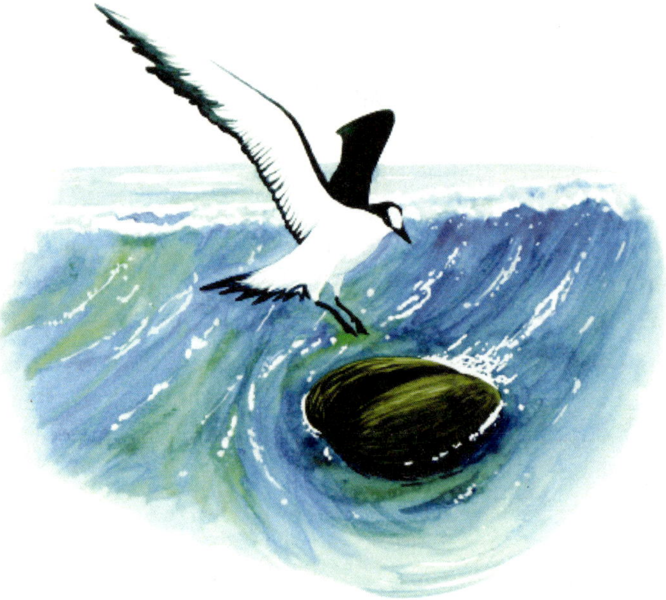

There's big – and then there's big!

Centuries ago, when wooden sailing ships crossed the Pacific Ocean, occasionally keen-eyed sailors would spot something floating in the water. On retrieving it, it would prove to be a nut; or more correctly, a double nut of a palm tree. And what a nut! Shaped like human buttocks, it proved to be the biggest seed in the world. But where could it have come from? No one knew. It began to be called the *coconut of the sea*. These early sailors thought that there must be a forest somewhere at the bottom of the sea and that these strange seeds had broken free and had floated up to the surface.

It was not until 1768 that this idea was put to rest when the source of these enormous seeds was discovered to be two islands in the Seychelles. These palm trees not only have the largest fruits in the world but – at up to seven metres long – they have the longest leaves too.

Intense pressure from collectors and damage from fire, as well as the introduction of many exotic plants throughout the islands, have severely curtailed regeneration of these unusual palms.

The *coco de mer* is now a protected species.

The 9000 km egg
Southern Africa

A small bird sheared across the slant of the sun. It was made smaller by the depth and width of the sky on every side. The drumming of its wings, its racing heart and brain and eye, drove the bird northwards and away from southern Africa. By evening, with the sun trailing its purple skirts against the lid of the Atlantic far to the left, the little bird slipped into the fierceness of the Kalahari Desert. Dawn came. The dry land stretched out before the bird as though there was no end to it. Then, far ahead, like a polished mirror thrown down onto a brown towel, Lake Ngami pulled into view. On the bird flew, not dropping down towards the lake and the comforts it would give but continuing across the water and across the great Okavango Swamps. Far beyond the swamplands she picked up the Zambezi and followed that river northwards until finally dropping height she came down to drink south of Senanga.

In Zaire she again came down out of the hot sky to drink. She landed on the edge of a small tributary, little more than a wide drain that emptied its store of mud water into the Kasai River. Small though it may be, this run of water was important to the little bird. She stayed for several days concealed among the reeds and hunted what insects were to be had there. She needed to store prodigious amounts of fat for the non-stop flight that she would now have to face. Once, a boy driving three goats came to the river to drink. Then he moved off again as suddenly as he had appeared. The bird returned to her feeding, eating many fat grubs and caterpillars. As though fearing what lay ahead she seemed reluctant to leave the safety and comfort of the small stream. But finally a day came when she again became restless. She tilted her beak upwards and springing into the air rose above the sanctuary of the tiny stream and turned northwards once more. This would be the most dangerous part of the journey. Not all birds would make it. Some would fall out of the sky from exhaustion. Some would be plucked from the air by hawks. The small bird did not know this. She only knew that she was compelled to move northwards, a speck against the sky.

Time passed in a dragging motion. Never faltering, the little bird – a cuckoo – at last crossed the equator. A small event in a busy world. The dark Congo River slipped away behind her. Far ahead lay the Central African Republic. Then it too lay behind her. She flew over Lake Chad. Was there no end to this journey? The Ahaggar Mountains – endless sand rose up to her as haze and rocky valleys. The shaded places among the scrub trees and reeds far back at the Kasai River were now a distant memory. Below there was nothing on which a bird could feed – nowhere a bird could drink. Only relentless sand, lonely as silence, sand hot enough to burn a bird's feet.

Suddenly, flying along the Algerian coast, the migrating bird felt a sharp jolt. She plunged erratically, falling down the sky and fighting to bring her wings back under control. Through her terror she glimpsed two boys far below staring up at her. One held a rifle. Renewed fear flushed across the bird's eyes. She could not fail, not now, not after so much effort. She must not fail. Ever alert to an attack from a hawk from above, she had not expected that anything would reach up to her from the ground. Slowly she brought her flying back under control and levelling her wings flashed out over the rolling Mediterranean Sea and away from the rapidly receding boys, now standing on top of a dune. The bullet had clipped the leading edges of two of her flight feathers.

Time was nothing. Flight was everything. Flying home was everything. The sun dragged itself upwards, then over, then down the high point in the sky. Only stars then, and a melon-slice of moon. Tiredness, with such heaviness now that it wanted to suck the bird out of the sky and smash her against the sea below. Her store of fat had long run to 'thin'. Fat was fuel. If her fuel choked empty she would spiral out of the sky.

Back in southern Africa the cuckoo had prepared well for her journey, had eaten many fat caterpillars. She had become fat-full and had sat around in a laze of good condition – waiting for the moment. What was the moment? Would she recognize it when it came? She didn't know any of this, didn't question any of it. But she had become unsettled. Three times she had risen out of her acacia bush only to settle down once more. The moment hadn't been right. Then the time came, a moment indistinguishable from the one that had gone before – indistinguishable except in the chemistry of the bird. She had lifted up out of the African heat and turned towards the north. The journey had begun that would lead her to a meadow pipit's nest on an island in the North Atlantic. Her mother before her had laid eggs in pipits' nests. This would prompt her, in her own turn, to seek, in preference, the nests of meadow pipits. She would lay one egg in each nest. But she first had to complete the dangerous journey.

Now, far from her acacia bush, the beat of her wings was her only companion. She could still fail and crash out of the sky. Below her endless land, then, finally, the Bay of Biscay. In darkness she passed over Bishop Rock and the Isles of Scilly. She could not see the ocean but she could smell the salt of the Atlantic. Endless ocean, ancient as time, indifferent to the plight of all small birds. A light – a lighthouse far ahead – guided the bird in the direction of her summer home. Without warning the rhythm in her wings that had been true for so long faltered. It wasn't much, but it was there. Fat was running dangerously low. Tiredness dragged at her muscles. It would be such an easy thing to give up. It would be such a release just to fold her wings and feel the cool stream of air rushing upwards and then the disintegration into the embrace of the unforgiving sea. Perhaps others in the darkness about her were crashing into the lead-grey of the heavy Atlantic water. Such a small splash they would make. Such a small disturbance – a slanting impact into the side of a wave to mark the end of a bird that had tried so hard. There were always failures on such a journey.

When the dawn came up again, the exhausted cuckoo crashed down into a soft field of sweet grass on the southeast coast of Ireland. One more cuckoo had made an astonishing 9000 km journey. When she had rested awhile she would seek to lay her eggs in the nests of other birds, one egg in each nest. These foster mothers would hatch her young and rear them as their own. It was now April. In July she would set off once more on her prodigious journey back to the land of her acacia bush. More astonishing still, her young, without guidance, would follow in September. That was for later. For now she would rest and eat, and watch meadow pipits – and bide her time.

Later on that very day, when the first of the cuckoos were slipping back into Ireland, Jerry McNeill and Paddy Brannigan leaned over a gate and looked into a field speckled about with young lambs. Suddenly, from the end of the field, the haunting double note of a cuckoo carried through the air. McNeill lifted his head in acknowledgement:

"That's the first I've heard this year," he said, and opened the gate to let a collie gather in the sheep.

"Summer has arrived when you hear the cuckoo," Brannigan said, and pointed the stem of his pipe in the direction from which the sound had come.

The return of the *cuach* quickened the rhythm of work in the farmlands of Ireland. Men who still had fields to be tilled hurried to put them under the plough. Any farmer caught sowing corn after the appearance of the African bird was saddled with the label of 'cuckoo farmer'. It had always been so when the unmistakable song of that strange bird carried across the Irish countryside.

The big guy in an English swamp

The frog hunkered down in a fat parcel of personality. He lounged about in self-assurance in a world forever frogs – and listened to the unfamiliar drone and cough of sound somewhere off to his left.

The big frog knew his marsh world. He knew where the water ran too deep and where it hipped up against a field of sheep. He knew where it seeped under a lemon-yellow umbrella of willow branches, where heavy cattle came to drink in summertime. He knew the now choked channel that had once drained the swamp into the River Ouse near Newton-on-Ouse some miles northwest of the ancient city of York.

He knew where tadpoles schooled like thunderclouds under a bin lid, now almost rusted through. In his day the lid had been new. Boys had skimmed it over the water from the sheep field. It had come to rest and got itself entangled among reeds at a depth of water unsafe for boys. They had repeatedly thrown stones at it. One heavy rock had hit the lid on one edge and flipped it over, dome-side up. When there was no more sport to be had from the lid, the boys left the swamp and never returned. But the lid remained. It tarnished to dullness and was rapidly skinned over with pondweeds.

The fat frog had been one of the first tadpoles born under the immense dome of the lid. He had seen generations of tadpoles and once a string of newt eggs spend important development time under the lid. He knew his swamp, but he did not know the strange chucking sound away off to his left.

But he knew other things. He knew the whereabouts of great diving beetles. These monsters were the nightmares of tadpoles, which were devoured alive with indifferent, scissor-like mouths. As an adult he had snapped at these monsters. Although he didn't like the bitter taste of the sour oil, he ate them when they came into his line of vision. He knew other things too. He knew where moorhens, black as charred reeds after fires, made their nests each year. He knew where jack pike seeped through forests of bulrushes to scald fear into frogs when it was too late.

The frog shifted about on his knot of marsh marigold leaves until everything sank a bit and he was more in than out of the water. In a haze of idleness he watched an out-of-range damselfly. The fly clung vertically to a single reed stalk, her tail barely dimpling the water. She clasped the stalk as though it was very precious. She seemed asleep. The blue markings on her wings did not say 'blue' to the frog; his world was of a different order. He registered movement, then shape. Many times he had eaten shapes like that, but here there was no movement other than the damselfly's dimpling of the water's surface with her tail. After a time of intense staring at the damselfly the frog became aware that something strange had occurred. The damselfly hadn't moved – of that he was sure – yet the end of her tail no longer touched the surface of the water.

In his lethargic world of contentment the frog's feelings drifted towards thoughts of Hanna. Until now the time had never been right. But recently something had changed that he would never understand. This evening Hanna would be covered by him. He would mount her and grasp her hard under the throat. They would half swim, half drift together. They would raft as a couple in a crowd of thousands under a cacophony of frog shrill rising up from across the entire swamp, frogs, in a world forever frogs, knowing that circumstances were now right. Reason enough for frog shrill.

The great frog would contribute sperm, and Hanna her eggs. The eggs would grow gelatinous and vibrant under the lid of the bin. Within a short time their tadpoles would join a new thundercloud of frog-life under the lid, safe there from the hypnotic stare of stilt-walking herons.

The frog stared again at the damselfly. Now the water lay lower still on the reed stalk. A damp stain on the stalk, where water had been, showed under the damselfly. Scrutinizing the damp patch the frog moved in an unsettled way on his simple raft of half-submerged leaves.

The sound that the frog had heard all day changed pitch. It grew lighter, less stressed. Then the excavator moved out of the reeds of the now freed channel. The iron teeth of the great machine dripped mud and silt – their day's work done.

The excavator hurried away in the direction of Newton-on-Ouse.

In wilderness is the way

It is common to talk of nature as though it is set aside from us, as something other than what we are. When we walk into a woodland we bring our presence with us. The woodland immediately undergoes a change by our being there. Birdsongs – jays', magpies' and blackbirds' – warn all of what has come among them. Other birds go silent and flit away. Animals, too, move back. What had but a moment before been an 'atmosphere' of woodland without humans is changed by our presence. Myriad things become more alert. Our intrusion is a felt thing that slips off through the trees.

Different forests display different comportments. Some are open and inviting, others are enfolded and closed. Those that are truly inviting are inspirational, like an open birch woodland in springtime. A place of white bark trees and fresh green canopy, with wave following wave of bluebells pushing back into the distance, is an invitation to dance with the joy of it all. Such woodlands are more than their appearance. We take from such places an echo that there is something deeper there than what we can see. If we could but sweep away what it is that conceals this deeper presence from us, we would experience a birch woodland in all its breathtaking complexity in a way that would force us to our knees in acknowledgement of the mystery of it all.

In such a woodland everything has its place, from the century-old trees to the leaf mould on which we walk. Such a forest is not a forest of trees alone, but the breath of deer, the movement of beetles under bark, the eyes of hawks staring downward, the webbing of spiders in numbers beyond count, the loose scales falling from the wings of butterflies, the snore of owls, the listening of mice, the streams of tree-life water moving up into the tallest canopy, the silence of fine snails slipping over wet grass, the hum of midwifeing insects, too numerous even to imagine. The very soil beneath our feet adjusts from one moment to the next to the movement of iron and potash, phosphorus and manganese and other minerals in their ceaseless upward precession to feed the swaying clouds of leaves above our heads. The intensity of the very breeze that flows past us is less or more than the day before and will differ again tomorrow because of the thickening of trees or the thinning of the woodland by the collapse of a monarch riddled with fungi. Even the strength of sunlight or rain coming down is different from one day to the next, when one more bud leafs out or two more leaves fall. And then we perceive a little, within the limits of what we can understand about such things, that no forest is identical with what it had been but a moment before. If we had eyes to comprehend it all we would truly see all forests as existing in a fog of continuous change, nothing remaining the same: a leaf less, a caterpillar more. And we too, surrounded by all of that transfiguration, are also changed. We walk from the woodland altered; and behind us, by our temporary presence within it, the woodland too has changed.

    I once had the privilege of an experience in a forest near the great St Lawrence River in Ontario. For several weeks I had been living in a hut in this forest. It was a simple wooden shack owned by some kind person unknown to me. He had left a notice on the door: *If you are a stranger and wish to use my hut please do so, and welcome.* The presence of that kind thought pinned to the door added greatly to the 'atmosphere' of that forest.

    I took up residence in that hut with three black rat snakes, a firm 'do not disturb' understanding in both camps. Living in that hut for that amount of time I got to know the forest in a way that would not be possible if I had been merely passing through and had dallied no more than a short while. Because of my extended stay I experienced the forest's silence with a greater intensity. Daily I encountered the endless hypnotic dance of flies in shafts of sunlight. Morning following morning they were there, the ceaseless energy of flies in their hum and weave of what it is to be flies in a shaft of sunlight coming down through trees. Pollen grains, too, in unimaginable numbers. They descended from tall conifers and rimmed yellow the puddles on the roadside with the sheer fecundity of their numbers. Other storms of pollen flecks high in the canopy drifted through the forest, so that at least some would carry their ancient information to the waiting female cones that new pines would follow.

On one particular and special day, standing in the silence of that forest, something happened. I seemed to slip into a condition that sportsmen describe as *the zone*. In this increased awareness all my perceptions were suddenly magnified. There had not been any effort on my part to bring this about. There was no trance state, no forced effort to seek enlightenment. I simply stood in that wonderful place without moving. An impenetrable hush moved down through the canopy above my head and I was in the zone. I understood then, with a comprehension that I had not known before, how all the dissimilar things that made up that great forest, be they bird or bush or bat, were all of the one thing. Nothing in that forest could stand outside of it all and be alone and independent of the rest. It would simply be incomplete without being part of the whole. Nothing was more important, or less important, than anything else. The entire forest – its trees and animals and birds, its fog of dust, its breath of leaves, its soak of water and minerals, its decay and its new life – was but one creation whole and indivisible, complete in itself; and standing among it all a solitary human now part of the same, trying without success to comprehend a mystery without dimension.

It is said that Japanese painters of the fifteenth century would go to a forest to paint. But they would paint nothing until they had spent several months there, taking from their surroundings what could not be expressed in words. Only then were they ready, only then was it time to set up the easels and take out the brushes. I imagine my experience was of a similar nature. But just as it had arrived unannounced, the experience moved away again, until I was left once more with my own limited awareness of what a forest is.

Down the years since then I have been in many forests but never again was I blessed with that incomprehensible encounter as I had near the great St Lawrence River those many years ago.

But wild lands, whether they are deep forests or heath lands or deserts, can, when we enter them, confer on us a heightened awareness of what we are in all our mystery. In such places we can see more clearly our presence in the world. Walking alone, with the rain buffeting against our faces, our concerns grow smaller. When we are troubled by deep personal difficulties these concerns become less in such places. We see them measured against the infinity of space and time. They become more manageable, and we can place them into a clearer perspective. There is value in wild places that can do that. Even if we have a deep illness, where the outcome is in doubt, a walk in a wild place can help to unravel our bundle of confused thoughts, discard what is not important, and assist us to accept with more equanimity the inevitable, if it is to be so. There is value in wild lands in this: in such places we come to understand that all things, ourselves too, have, for a time, an existence – then no existence. In such places we can see what is often hidden from us in towns and cities, that our lives – and then our non-existence – are part of a wonderful, mysterious, natural process. There is value in wild places in this. A reason that we protect them from destruction.

Jamaica drift [1]

Jamaica and Scotland

The northeast trade winds press against the Blue Mountains in the high interior of Portland, Jamaica. Rain falls from low clouds and feeds itself in streams into the Rio Grande. Parts of that great river run smooth and straight, while other sections ripple and swing through canyons and gorges. On the banks grow enormous vines. Of these, the entada climbs thirty metres into the canopy of tall trees and produces seed-pods worthy of its size. These pods are similar in appearance to those on broad beans, except that on the entada they grow to a metre in length. On occasion some of these pods fall into the Rio Grande. They get carried downstream as debris to be deposited on sandbanks, or shunted into backwater eddies to circle endlessly in the vagaries of that world. But some are carried further. Now and then one of these bean pods floats all the way to the mouth of the Rio Grande and floods out into the Caribbean Sea.

For a time the pod drifts without direction. Then the movement of the North Equatorial Current takes it into its domain and carries it westward. The bean pod drifts for days. Days become weeks and the pod slips through the Yucatan Channel. Held firmly now in the grip of this new force, a force that runs a mile deep and with a volume of several hundred Mississippi rivers, the pod moves northwards, then towards the east, following the coastline of Cuba. Finally it enters the main swath of the Florida Current and tracks up the coastline of North America as far as Cape Hatteras.

Beyond Cape Hatteras the warm sixty-million-year-old

Gulf Stream confronts the cold Labrador Current ploughing out of the frigid waters of Baffin Bay. The green northern waters contest the right of passage and deflect the blue waters of the Gulf Stream eastward. The giant pod, waterlogged, barely afloat, drifts away from the coast of North America. Saturated through with salt water, the pod fragments somewhere in the dense fog east of the Grand Banks. Hard seeds spill into the ocean. The remains of the pod and two of the seeds sink into the depths of the North Atlantic. Still afloat, a handful of brown seeds drift together in the immensity of that huge ocean. With the passing of a month, what had been a tight cluster of entada seeds becomes dispersed over several square kilometres of the North Atlantic Drift. Two more seeds sink.

For nearly a year the remaining entada seeds drift in the ocean. It seems as if there is no end to this North Atlantic. Seven seeds still remain afloat, three of them barely so. A storm comes out of the southwest and boils the heaving swell into terrible rollers. The remaining entada seeds are carried down into the steep-sided troughs to rise again up the next green wall of water. Three further seeds sink. Ahead a serrated landmass shears up out of the half dark. One mountainous wave rolls forward, feeling the drag of the gathering shallows beneath it. It raises itself higher; spindrifts – like wild grey hair – stream back from its head. Finally the heavy wave keels over and explodes up a rock-strewn beach. For a moment the enormous wave lies spent and broken on the land. Then, with a grating, dragging sound, the wave claws itself back down the slope to the sea. The dead wave gullets in the smooth rocky channels that are neither of the sea nor of the land. In the wake of the wave, high on the storm beach, lies a solitary entada bean. It had taken sixteen months of ocean drift. That single bean from the Rio Grande had survived the ocean journey.

In the following summer a child from Edinburgh on holiday with his parents on the Isle of Mull discovered the bean while hunting for sea urchins. He brought it home rolled up in a sock. In Scotland, in the last century, finding a 'fiery egg' or 'sea bean' brought good luck to the finder. Such beans were worn as charms; indeed, pregnant women thought they would prevent miscarriages. But when the child brought the strange bean back to Edinburgh no one knew of these things. No one knew what the bean was. They did not know of the heroic journey. The bean was placed on the mantelpiece. Against the odds it was still alive. Two months later the entada bean was thrown into the fire.

1. Based on a paper by Dr E. C. Nelson: 'Tropical drift fruits and seeds on coasts in the British Isles and Western Europe: 1. Irish Beaches', *Watsonia* 12, pp. 103-112 (1978).

Salamander

A salamander on a rock. Feet up, feet down, turn about, watch. Such is the nature of a salamander. Always on the watch. If we don't move she won't see us. But you mustn't move. If you move she'll skitter off under stones.

There she goes again. Feet up, feet down, turn about, watch. Colours change. Other than that she divulges nothing of what it is to be a salamander.

Movement in front of her – all legs, all undulations drawing towards her. She cracks open the beetle.

"Did you see the speed of that?"

Movement again – up, down, turn about – gone. Empty rock.

"You moved."

"No, you moved!"

Such a thing is a salamander.

Tiger day
India

The huge cat roared its anger. It roared its anger out of its wildness, out of what it was to be a tiger, the last living tiger on the planet.

Already, in Berkeley, glass bottles of the animal's blood plasma lay entombed in liquid nitrogen. Semen from the tiger was deep-frozen in an aluminium flask. Recordings, countless recordings, of the sounds of the last tiger had been made. There was nothing more that they could take, except one thing – and they would take that today in full view of a watching world.

To Charan Chandra, the leader of the group that held the tiger, this animal was more precious than any diamond dug out of an African mine. It was more precious than gold. It was more precious than any computer chip. The tiger was part of the high art of the planet. The life that flowed under the skin of the great cat was the final account of three million years of tiger evolution. This life would not evolve further. It could not evolve further. Through the advancement of science it might, in time, be given a ghost existence, but never again would it be a tiger in the fierce quality of what it was to be a big cat.

They had chosen a mud bank some distance out in the Bay of Bengal on which to hide the animal. The huge Simlipal National Park that had contained the last of the tigers lay to their west. For three weeks the police and the army of the Indian government had searched for the four men and one woman who held the last tiger in captivity. It seemed as if all of India was engaged in the search. Finding the tiger had become a national issue. The story grew. It became of world interest. No one had thought to search the off-shore mud banks. The four men and the woman had counted on that. The boats that had brought the great cage and the television crew and the powerful transmitters to the mud bank now lay hidden under a cloak of leaves and silt. Against the possibility of air reconnaissance the cage had been draped in a shroud of camouflage netting.

The three men that made up the television crew sat some distance removed from the others and from the cage. They sat under the shade of a tree on the edge of the water. The heat was intense. They talked together in low tones. They speculated on what was to happen at noon. Their CNN bosses had given them the nod to go. The men, with their equipment stored in two crates, had boarded a plane for India – and dropped out of sight.

Secrecy had been the deal. During the night, the television crew had set up their transmitting equipment. Now everything was ready. If it went as planned the signals would be picked up and broadcast around the world. For days every newspaper in India and every major newspaper across the world carried the news of the hunt for the group holding the last tiger on earth. If they weren't captured by Wednesday then something dramatic would happen at noon on that day. No one could say what would happen. That made the search more urgent. That made viewing compulsory. Television stations around the world vied for the rights to re-transmit the signal. All was now ready. It was Wednesday – twenty minutes to noon.

The four men and one woman sat together beside the tiger cage. They did not speak. They sat gazing out across the brown-stained waters of the Bay of Bengal. The tiger crouched uneasily in the shrouded cage. Time clawed towards noon. The heat intensified. Twice the leader of the group looked at his watch. Then it was time.

"Right, let's do it," he said.

He stood up and stripped the camouflage netting from the cage. The tiger swirled like yellow smoke, exploded against the bars and struck out with electrifying speed at the man. But Charan Chandra knew tigers. He knew the way of tigers.

For twenty-seven years Charan Chandra had worked to save the biggest cats on earth. As Tiger Warden in the Simlipal National Park he had worked with politicians. He had worked to persuade them, to coax them. He had worked with the hill people; he had worked with their elders. He had talked with conservation agencies. He had talked *through* conservation agencies to wider audiences. He had talked to protect the tigers. He had talked of the need to give space to tigers on this planet. The Bali tiger had become extinct. So too had the Javan and Caspian tigers. All agreed – such a fine animal as the Bengal tiger! – wouldn't it be a shame! No one said *what* would be a shame.

Years before, fine reserves had been set aside and designated as land where tigers could live. That was more like it! 'Save the Tiger' became the new catchword. Tigers increased in numbers. People were pleased. Politicians were pleased. They were pleased to be associated with the fine project. International conservation agencies said that "this is what conservation is all about."

But people too had needs. Poor people had needs. They needed land. They filtered into the land of the tiger. No harm done – just a little piece of land out of such a large amount. The lands of the tiger were big; more people came. They sifted like shadows through the trees. They sought out little patches of ground where they could grow food and keep a cow. They did not take big pieces of the land of the tiger, they took small pieces. But there were many people. There seemed to be no end to the flow of people coming into the land of the tiger.

Then it happened. It should not have surprised anyone when it did. A tiger took a goat from the edge of a small village. When a second goat was taken people said that something had to be done. They had worked hard to clear little patches of land to provide for their families. They could not afford the loss of a goat. They came together as a group and went into the forest and killed a tiger. On their return the hunters showed their trophy and said that this was the tiger that had taken the goat. When a calf was taken, and a cow was taken three days later, people said that *something had to be done*. A week after the cow had been killed a seven-year-old boy was sent gathering sticks. He never returned from the forest. People said it had to be a tiger that had killed the boy. The villagers went into the strongholds of the tigers and killed tigers.

Zoos across the world had once kept tigers. Then people had said that zoos should not keep tigers. It was not right that such fine animals should be kept in zoos. They should be allowed to run free in their natural home. Zoos then no longer kept tigers; tiger reserves were the answer. And they *were* the answer – until the people came. One by one each tiger reserve was overrun by people. It was overrun by poor people who had need of small patches of land where they could rear a family. In time there was but a single tiger reserve left in all of India and the world. When the villagers, who had set up homes illegally in the last tiger sanctuary, went to the strongholds of the tigers on the death of the boy, a solitary male animal had escaped the hunting parties. Time and again the villagers had gone into the forest to hunt down the roar of the last tiger on Earth, but no one had succeeded.

Charan Chandra had stayed awake for many nights. He thought on the plight of the last tiger. If even a pair of animals had escaped the villagers ... but when there was only one! Then Charan Chandra went cold with anger. He had spent his life winning a place for tigers in India. He had listened to assurances He had even believed them. He had listened to proclamations of intent that would "once and for all guarantee a place for tigers." Twice he had been shot at. A colleague had been killed protecting tigers. He thought hard on these things. He thought again of the solitary tiger somewhere in the dark forest north of where he lay. Finally Charan Chandra decided what he must do. Then he went to sleep.

Ten days later the team of five had baited a trap in the dark forest. All that day and all the following night the rain roared down. But the tiger did not come. In the darkness of the fourth night the hair on Charan Chandra's neck tingled. His years of contact with tigers had given him an unexplained sense. He listened against the drumming of the rain. Not a sound could he hear. Minutes passed. A wet shadow. Perhaps it was nothing at all. The shadow again, off to his right – barely there. Suddenly almond eyes in the rain. A flash of movement. A terrible shuddering in the net. The roar of the last tiger rang out through the wet forest. It disturbed, for the last time, the sambar deer in their sleep; the treepies too would miss the tiger passing by. One of the team administered the drug. The xylazine sponged the rage of power out of the big cat. When finally it dropped into sleep they shunted the huge animal into the strong cage.

Now, three weeks later, the cage sat on the mud island. Charan Chandra nodded to the cameramen. It was time. The men clambered to their feet. When their cameras and transmitters were ready they gave the signal to go.

Charan Chandra stood by the cage. The tiger turned its head. It stared at the man out of the narrowing flints of its eyes. It crouched tight to the floor. The tail moved rhythmically, ears flattened against the broad skull. A low spitting growl warned Charan Chandra. Suddenly the huge cat, exploding forward with terrifying speed, slashed a great paw out through the bars of the cage and at the face of Charan Chandra. But Charan Chandra knew the way of tigers. Once again the tiger retreated to the back of the cage.

The group had constructed a wooden podium on the mud bank to give dignity to the occasion. This they now took from among the trees and placed on the mud beside the cage. Charan Chandra stepped onto the podium. The other members of the group took their places behind him. At exactly noon the transmission began. The signal was picked up by satellite and relayed around the world.

"My name is Charan Chandra," he said. Then he turned and trailed his fingers in the direction of the young woman: "Dr Marie Black, veterinary surgeon from New Hampshire, USA." He bowed his acknowledgement in the direction of the woman in the green cotton shirt and slacks. Then his fingers swept out to identify in turn the two well-built men in khaki shirts and shorts. "Jack Hamilton and Sam Fisher, game biologists from Kruger National Park." Sam Fisher half raised his arm in acknowledgement. "The final member of our group is Zack Zelderman, the well-known poet and philosopher." The slender brown fingers of Charan Chandra trailed out towards the poet. The familiar face of the huge New Zealander flooded into the camera. When each member of the group had been introduced, Charan Chandra turned back towards the camera. For a long moment he remained silent, staring into the lens. Then he said in a firm voice: "I want to tell you about tigers."

He told his worldwide audience how as a boy he had listened to his grandfather's beautiful stories of Indian tigers. When he had been old enough he had been taken by his father to the Mundanthurai Tiger Reserve where he had seen his first tiger. Later his father had taken him to the Ranthambhore National Park in Rajasthan, to see the tigers of northern India. The memory of those days had stayed with him, he said. He talked of the past, of the splendid hunting parties that had gone out to kill tigers. He talked of the once fashionable trade in tiger fur. He talked of the trade in the very bones and whiskers of the animal. Above all he talked of the unstoppable tide of people who had come and settled on the land of the tigers. Then he turned and looked at the animal in the cage.

"Now there is a single tiger left in the world."

The cameraman panned slowly towards the great cage. The tiger prowled. It rippled and snarled in its anger. People around the world stared. Most had never seen a tiger. They had seen tigers in storybooks. They had seen them in documentary films. But this was different. This was the last living tiger on earth. Fathers lifted their children onto their knees and said:

"That is a tiger. That is a very rare animal."

The children stared at the magical animal.

"Would he bite, daddy?" one of the children asked.

"Bite? He'd eat you all up," daddy said, and gave his little girl a hug.

"Oooh," she said, delighted that she was safe with daddy. She stared at the magical animal that could eat you all up. It was as big as a dragon would be, and just as fierce. It was as magical as a rhinoceros – when there had been rhinoceroses.

All of India, it seemed, had, for once, stopped its eternal bustle and had gathered about innumerable television sets to see the last Indian tiger. They were proud. It was their tiger and the entire world was looking at their Indian tiger. Not just in India, but also across the whole sprawl of Asia lying to the north, and in Africa and in Europe people stared at the image of the huge animal. Americans and Australians, too, stared at the last tiger. No one knew what was going to happen. For days the newspapers had speculated. The team of five had planned it that way. They had planned for maximum impact. The difficult weeks of avoiding the Indian soldiers were over.

Now the camera panned back to Charan Chandra. He lifted his hands and in resignation presented his palms to the world:

"There is no room any more for tigers on this planet," he said. "There is no room, just as there was no room for Cape lions or for Japanese wolves or for blue buck. So why do we continue the charade?" He turned and faced the tiger again. The animal snarled quietly. "We don't want tigers. We may wish to have tigers – but that is not the same as want." He stared into the camera again. "Want demands obligation. In the end, through all the fog of words, there was no commitment to protecting tigers." He pointed the tips of his fingers at the cage. "Now we are reduced to one tiger. What are we to do with this animal? It represents all that is and was – tiger. We cannot let it roam free to become old and to finally die in a ravine – the last of the tigers to walk the forests of India. That would not be right. The whimpering of an old animal should finally not represent millions of years of tiger roar."

People around the world nodded in agreement. It would not be right that such a beautiful animal should simply be turned out into the jungle to die of old age.

On the signal of Charan Chandra, the four members of his group went to the cage. Sam Fisher undid the lock and opened the door, but only to a degree that allowed Jack Hamilton to slip a long steel pole inside. Chains held the door of the cage from opening further. The tiger spat and struck out at the tip of the pole where the hook was. The pole crept towards the powerful neck. A steel collar, with a metal ring, had already been placed around the neck of the animal. The hook slipped into the metal ring and locked.

Then, very slowly, very quietly, Dr Marie Black from New Hampshire, USA, undid the chains on the door. Sam Fisher and Jack Hamilton held the steel pole and braced themselves. Zack Zelderman eased open the door and stood back.

Smouldering eyes stared from the cage straight at Charan Chandra. On the nod from Charan Chandra the two men holding the steel pole took a step backwards, then a second. They tightened their grip on the pole. One more step. The animal exploded into a fury and slashed out at the pole and scored claw marks along the hard steel. Struggling to contain the fierceness of the huge cat, the men inched back one more step. The hook on the heavy pole dragged at the steel collar, forcing the tiger forward. Taking them by surprise, the animal then stalked quietly through the door of the cage and stepped down onto the mud of the island. Never once did the tiger's eyes leave the face of Charan Chandra. The camera crew glanced at each other and screwed their nerves down into hard knots. They tracked the movement of the huge cat.

Around the world people crowded closer to their television sets. This was the last tiger on earth. They stared at the beautiful creature and at all of that ferocity. They were amazed at the unbelievable bravery of the small group confronting the animal. A man in Bergen said out loud that he had once seen a tiger in a zoo in Oslo. He was told to be quiet so that they could watch what was going to happen.

"God, it's far bigger than the cougars which used to live round here," a certain Dan Casey said. He stared at the moose head on the cabin wall. He stared again at the 318 kg tiger and waved his arm at the windows and at the sprawl of New Mexico outside. "Christ, he's bigger than any cougar."

The tiger flared again. Charan Chandra shouted at the tiger and clapped his hands to draw its attention away from the cameramen and to focus its attention on him alone. He stood directly in front of the tiger, no more than twenty metres from the animal. The tiger roared at Charan Chandra. Charan Chandra shouted at the tiger. The tiger roared. It crouched low to the mud. It fed the distance between it and Charan Chandra into its understanding. It kneaded the wet mud with enormous claws and judged the distance. Very slowly Charan

Chandra nodded his head. His eyes remained rigidly fixed on the crouching tiger. Sam Fisher, sweat streaming down his face and struggling to hold the big cat, eased back on the wire that ran the length of the pole. The heavy hook fell away from the steel collar. The animal was free.

Sensing its freedom the cat scraped at the ground. With ears flat to its skull, it judged the distance. Then, with terrible speed, the tiger streaked through the air, was all tiger in the freedom of being a tiger, all fierceness in the way a tiger is fierce – the last of the tigers in the full glory of what it was to be a tiger. A single shot rang out.

Charan Chandra rolled sideways. The tiger crashed dead where the man had stood but a moment before. Nobody had noticed the powerful rifle that Charan Chandra had slipped from his smock. The cameramen were stunned. People around the world were stunned. Fathers turned their children's faces away. The famous warden who loved tigers, who protected tigers, had shot the last tiger in existence.

The tiger had not gone quietly into the Great Fade. It had gone in the glory of what it was *to be a tiger* – and the world had watched and would have to deal with its guilt.

Charan Chandra placed his rifle beside the dead animal. He quietly sat down on the mud close to the tiger. The four other people sat down beside him. They watched the necklace of military boats drawing closer across the Bay of Bengal. The year was 2030.

Echoes in the sea

A blue whale, the largest creature on earth, is a tiny thing against the immensity of the length and breadth and depth of the oceans. We are told that 8,000 to 14,000 blue whales exist. Once there were 250,000 – we are told. Today the strange songs of these creatures rarely echo in the canyons of the sea. Some calls are sterile, trumpeting through the dark to turn great whales that no longer exist. There is diminishing music in the sea that once pulsed with choirs of whales.

Today, we no longer kill whales with harpoons. We kill them with *research*. In an age depleted of blue whales, what judgement of us moves in the brains of these magnificent animals? Brains that know the passes through the mountains of the great oceans; that have confronted giant squid; that have seen the wrecks of whaling ships – are they aware that something has changed? Are they aware that fewer great whales inhabit the seas? Are they aware how few?

Will it matter if there is silence in the ocean of whales?

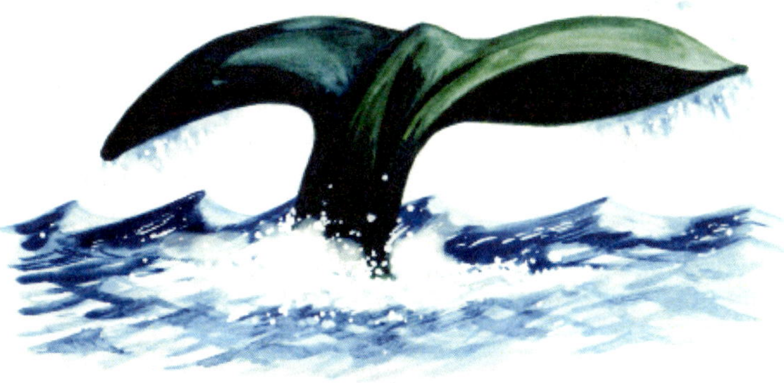

Silence in Madagascar

The circumference around the long axis is to be 89 cm. The circumference around the middle is to be 73 cm. The colour of the surface is to be brownish but fading in patches, and the surface is to be slightly stippled. One other thing – children are to be allowed to touch the egg. Any colouring, therefore, must be added to the material itself and not simply applied to the surface, because otherwise it will get rubbed off by many small hands.

These were the instructions I gave to an artist who would make an elephant bird's egg as part of an exhibition I was creating in a bird reserve. As well as the egg, we made, to scale, a cut-out of a full-size elephant bird. In life such a bird stood over three metres tall and weighed just under five hundred kilogrammes.

Not able to fly, it was, however, armed with massive claws and a fierce beak and was well able to defend itself. What a jaw-dropping and terrifying experience it must have been for Dutch and Portuguese sailors when walking through the forests of Madagascar to suddenly come across this giant. Some of these sailors brought eggs of this magnificent bird to Europe. The equivalent of two hundred hen eggs in size, these giant eggs were a wonder to behold.

The existence of these birds is recorded in the memoirs of Marco Polo and may have been the basis for the story of the Giant Roc in *Sinbad the Sailor*.

It is not known with certainty when elephant birds became extinct. It is likely that they had died out by the year

1700. And with their passing the world truly lost something special.

The elephant birds have left us their silence. In the end it was all they had left to give.

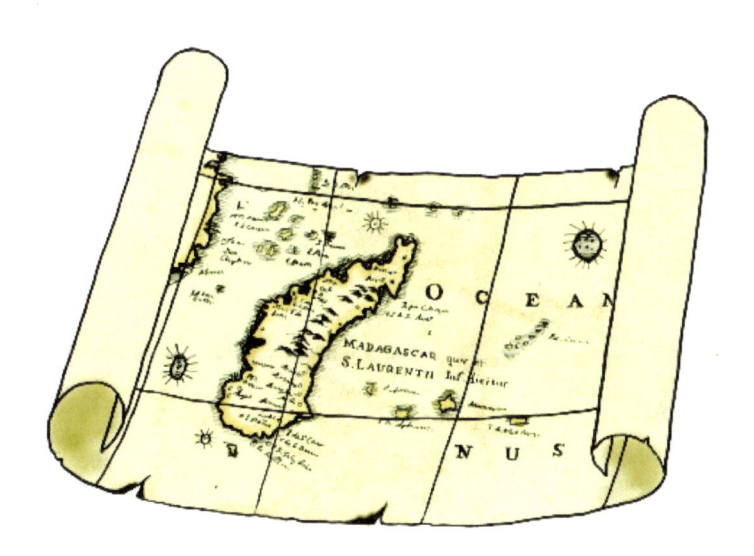

PART II

So what might we – all of us – do to protect the biodiversity of this planet?

Meeting again with old friends

We are losing species. Beautiful animals and plants are going into the fade – then into the nothing.

Where are our Japanese wolves? Once we could see against the sky our Carolina parakeets, our yellow-headed macaws, our painted vultures. Where are they now? Where are our Palestinian painted frogs, and the wine palms of the Dominican Republic?

There have always been extinctions, some indeed on a huge scale. Now, however, there is something different – we are a factor in extinctions. We do not need to quote statistics here. Others have already done that in numerous books and reports. There is no necessity to give reasons for these extinctions. Others, too, on numerous occasions, have listed the reasons. It is sufficient to admit that things are not as they should be. But before we can begin to attempt to make things better we need to rethink our relationships to nature.

We must approach this calmly. There is too much hysteria and there are too many doomsayers around the issues of conservation. In strident tones many attempt to provoke us to change our ways. I have never been convinced that demonstrations of indignation or raised voices can compel us to change. Something different is needed.

Centuries ago, those who were us then lived their lives close to nature. They were aware of bear prints and wolf prints and the slots of deer in snow. They were acutely conscious of sounds; the sounds of crickets and of bats at night, and the suck of a salmon at evening time. They were familiar with the velvet swish of mice through dry grass and were aware of the speck of a kestrel hovering at an astounding height above their heads. They observed the ghost-passage of barn owls through woods at evening time. They could point out where a wild pig had feasted on beech mast and where underground seas of bulbs send up vast armies of bluebells in the springtime of the year. Whether it was the warning of high geese at the coming of the first frost or the quickening pace of dormice at leaf fall, these, our people back then, had a keen awareness of things around them.

But that is now changed. We have uncoupled ourselves from all of this. Where the countryside had been a place of wilderness, now it is a place of production. Things that are wild have been moved away from our lives. We have created great cities but we have not extended a hand to nature and invited her in as an old friend. A fox in a city park creates a stir. A peregrine nesting on the high cliff face of a skyscraper gets her picture taken for 'Other news'. We now largely know of wildlife through books and television programmes. There is an unbridgeable difference in experience between reading about the warm smell of lion cubs, fat as ivy berries, and holding a bunch of them in our arms. The difference is one of proximity to the real.

So, what is it that we need to do? We need to find in our lives a place for nature. We need to meet again with old friends. If we do this, then many conservation problems will fall away. And how might we again draw close to things that were once familiar?

No guilt

I believe that we are essentially good. We mean well even though sometimes we get things horribly wrong. We are also creative people, inventing things for our benefit. On occasion some of our inventions produce consequences that nobody could have predicted. Scientific methodology and double-blind tests allow us to travel only part of the journey along the road of consequence. The rest is risk. Who could have predicted that we would be capable of damaging the ozone layer or be capable perhaps of changing the climate of the world? Neither was deliberate, both are disturbing eye-openers.

At this stage some are tempted to point fingers. Some do point fingers. When all the pointing is done – what then? Part of the cost of the car you drive, part of the cost of the car I drive, is in the dead plankton in the sea and in the fewer bird songs carried on the wind. Each of us carries our share of these problems. "Yes," you say, "but he more than I." That's finger pointing. We need to move from this position. We need to admit mistakes – terrible mistakes on occasion – then move to improve things, and do so without guilt or rancour or finger pointing.

Industries are judged on the look of a ledger sheet. Managers are judged on profit. Efficiency is the needle that prods all forward. A spike on the stock market is the applause for success. It confers bonuses on those in charge. That's business.

It might be said that accountants and engineers are precise people. They abhor uncertainty. These fine qualities make bridges stand up, dams hold together and budgets come in as intended. Nothing is left to chance. These are good disciplines that give comfort to project chiefs. Accountants and engineers are men and women who get the job done. Nothing tacky in their thinking. In a world of complex decisions such people are often the few who appear to deal in certainty. An engineer can tell how many million cubic metres of cement and aggregate will be needed to build a proposed dam. He will calculate the amount of electricity the finished dam will generate. Accountants will reveal the costs of the construction of the dam and the returns from the sale of the electricity. Laudable qualities. A lot of certainty there.

Let's have a big hand for the engineers and for the accountants – except that in all projects there are 'unquantifiables', factors that cannot be measured on a spreadsheet or captured in a draughtsman's drawing. What can't be quantified tends to be ignored – the neat mind at play! Imponderables, if allowed to trail through a report, would fog the issues. They would render it difficult for managers to reach decisions. They would imply that the report lacked crispness. The presence of imponderables would blunt the strength of the recommendations on offer. In the end the quality of the report writer would be put in question. Best for all that no fog looms over the pages. And how might that be done?

Startlingly simple. Unquantifiables are judged to be outside economic arguments. And there's the rub. What can be measured is deemed important, what cannot is of the quality of mist. And that distinction puts nature in harm's way. Reports may on occasion allude to imponderables. These may be tucked under 'other considerations'. They may be offered as footnotes. Sometimes they are ignored, the report staying silent on the matter.

And what are these mysterious imponderables? Our simple case of the construction of the dam might be taken as an example. The dam might flood a water meadow, drowning out the flowers that grow there, flowers that give joy to children at flower-picking time. This reduction in the pleasure of a child is part of the cost of the dam construction that does not feature in the spreadsheet. So too is the submergence under the rising water of a hazel woodland on which mice and squirrels have depended for food. Fewer mice will affect owl and fox and wolf populations. But the fine dam will result in an increase in fish and eel and frog numbers. Herons will benefit from this and their population will rise to a new level of sustainability. This positive effect is also an imponderable.

There are also more invidious effects entangled within the costs of production of most things. Industrial residue seeping into a river is efficiency – to a factory owner or to a farmer. It eliminates cleaning expenses from the 'costs of production'. This stealth deportation helps the spreadsheet shine more brightly. It also kills fish. It kills the enjoyment of fishermen. It robs the excitement from a child's eye seeking to see a great salmon. It puts a crimp in hotel bookings. Fewer sportsmen lean across tackle-shop counters to discuss copper lures or mayfly rigs. These imponderables, these lost opportunities to others, often register as zero costs to the factory owner or to the farmer.

In addition there are other consequences that lie further back in the fog. The disappearance of butterflies, the decline in caddis fly numbers, the sickness in the bellies of hedgehogs which have eaten too many poisoned snails. So many snails about that evening, it had been all too easy – and one more hedgehog lies dying.

An interesting question might be raised here. Where do the true boundaries of a farm lie? Do they remain at the farm gate or five miles downriver where the last residue of pig waste settles among stones? Do they extend fifteen wind-driven miles to where the few remaining molecules of a pesticide do not disturb the hover flies? The true costs of modern farming include the subtleties of a thousand things disturbed.

Other negative factors carried in the wind come like stealth creatures to chip and dissolve away the paint on our windows. They corrode our iron and stone monuments, kill our trees and sometimes ourselves. These effects, too, are not factored into the costs of modern industries or modern farming. These costs are absorbed by the community in the extra tin of paint that is needed, or in the price to replace a dead shrub, or in the sorrow for a loved one going before their time.

In the end it is impossible to quantify the true costs of the production of anything. Indeed some consequences may not reveal themselves until decades later, and even then some of these may only show their claws half a globe away in the lichens of the High Arctic or in the fat of fur seals. Like wet snow on a roof, the art and certainty of accounting falls away at this point. Attempting to put costs on all the imponderables would prove as illusive as the quest for zero-point energy or an understanding of tetraneutrons. But we should at least acknowledge their existence.

So where can we go from here? Well, the first thing we need to admit is that business is the business of profit. Without profit there is no business. In the discipline of business there is scant room for sentiment. Indeed, we are told not to let emotions cloud our judgements. This is an extraordinary demand on us. We are sentient beings riddled through with whole battalions of emotions. We reach pinnacles of elation when our home team hits the winning score and sees the others off the pitch. We groan in dismay, wave our fists, cry even, when the same team throws it all away on one ill-considered move. With the power of his music Wagner curls our toes. Mozart leads us into a world of sublime beauty. Then Beethoven changes it all by having us up on our feet conducting the air to the cathedral-like waterfall of music that speaks of the triumph of men and the triumph of nature. Day-old chickens and tiny kittens compel small children to pick them up. In witnessing a swan losing her mate we are moved to deep sadness. The stillness of ancient glaciers rams humility into our souls. We stare at galaxies, at the mind-numbing distances and the stupendous measurements of time they represent, and fall silent before it all. Yet all of these wonderful human qualities we are expected to leave outside the boardroom door and debate business only from logic and efficiency. We look down at our plastic reflections staring back at us out of the polished corporate table and make clever decisions on how to increase production – with no mention of the decline of frogs or the diminution of wonderment in a child's eye that will be a consequence of what we intend to do. Adulthood, it appears, is serious time when serious things must be achieved. Little else is allowed a seat at the table. This closing down of our emotional side during these decision-making processes endangers wildlife.

Some species lose completely by what we do, and disappear. In the process we too lose something. We lose an opportunity to be intrigued and to be fascinated by things that once were. Where have the bee-eaters of the Hawaiian Islands gone? Where are their songs, their exquisite colours? We remember their names, in the way we remember the names of soldiers lost in old battles. But where are their nests? Where are their young? We are the poorer for the absence of these things. Passenger pigeons once triggered awe and wonder in those who saw them, not because of their quiet beauty but because they flocked together in their tens of millions. They congregated in numbers so vast that a single flock passing over a village community would darken the sky for hours. These extraordinary happenings are now folk memories. The bird is extinct. As a consequence, one more opportunity is denied us to stand in astonishment before an extraordinary event of nature.

Years ago I used to work as a naturalist in Canada, giving talks to visitors in parks and park campsites. The ambition behind the talks of the naturalists was to lead park visitors, both adults and children, towards a heightened appreciation of the value of nature in our lives. From this it was hoped that they would take home with them a more responsible attitude towards wildlife. It is true that many times we fell short of what we hoped to achieve. On a rare occasion a naturalist of exceptional ability might draw his or her audience close to a revelation of the wholeness and undividedness of all life, but such moments are exceptional.

I found these talks most satisfying. Perhaps my audiences were being kind, but I got the impression that they enjoyed what I had to say. For my part I hoped that they had learned a little from what we discussed, so, to that degree at least, these talks might be judged a success. But at the more ambitious level of attempting to change adult minds to a more responsible attitude towards nature – I'm not so sure I achieved anything at all. I have questioned people on this. I have talked to them six months or a year after they had attended some of my talks. Yes, they found the talks informative, entertaining even, but no, their behaviour towards nature had not changed. One of the reasons given was the hard reality of the pace of life. People are too busy. They are attempting to do well at their jobs and to run their homes and rear their children and have little time to reflect on the circumstances of their own lives, never mind anything else. This swirl of activity seems to go with the territory of adulthood. I have now come to the conclusion that it is not possible to change adult minds in this fashion. Of course there are always exceptions and some may indeed change their attitudes but I maintain that what I say here is essentially true.

Children's minds, on the other hand, appear to be much more open to change. I feel that here we are on much more fertile ground. Children can be persuaded to change their views, and if such views are carried into adulthood, then park programmes aimed at children can be of enormous benefit to wildlife conservation. If, therefore, our programmes of nature talks are failing in their primary objective, should we not review what we are doing and re-focus our work almost exclusively on children?

When we step away from childhood, we seem to step away from the awareness of nature we held to be important when we were small. The scuttling of crabs across bits of shells, the clouds of sand hoppers that scattered before our feet – things that once filled us with excitement – become dull and uninteresting when we leave our childhood behind. Yet these things pre-date our own existence by millions of years. They are our origins. Where once the cry of a seagull was big and important to a child, it becomes in adulthood a half-heard thing that disturbs serious conversation. We may walk the same woods we walked as children, but as adults we see only at the scale of trees and boulders and the dog running ahead of us. We no longer notice the delicate and the small.

Because of this detachment, this slippage into indifference, regulations that may look fine on paper will not in the end protect wildlife. Something more is required. What is missing is a 'want' that nature should not be damaged by what we do. Only when this 'want' becomes widespread will the needs of the 'imponderables in the fog' start to be addressed.

Are all species 'useful'?

Now there's a question!

It is interesting to speculate: if dinosaurs, as dinosaurs, had survived to modern times, would they have been of any use to us? Parts of their blood might have turned out to be exceedingly valuable in medicine as thinning or as clotting agents. Their eggs might have shown extraordinary nutritious qualities and be particularly rich in protein. We might have extensive dinosaur egg-producing units scattered across the globe. Prudence would prompt selecting small herbivore species – to keep life insurance costs within manageable limits! All of this is of course speculation. We will never know the potential 'usefulness' that was lost to us sixty-five million years ago.

This brings us to the usefulness of species alive today; we need to acknowledge that we do not know the full potential of *any* species. I am sure that this is true. Equally, we cannot say with certainty that any species is 'useless'. There is not a single organism, whether it is an HIV or a smallpox virus or a bacterium, about which we can say with certainty that it will never be of value to us in the future. So we need to be careful, if only for selfish reasons, that a species is not driven to extinction by what we do.

I have on my desk a small glass bottle. Inside, immersed in preservative fluid, is a small rat-tail fish. Such a strange creature is found at the depth where the *Titanic* now lies at rest. I am told that this little fish may hold curative potential for some forms of cancer. I do not know if this is so, but if a fish from two miles down can prove of use to us then surely any species may well hold as yet unknown benefits.

Indeed, we repeatedly return to wild species to improve

our cultivated varieties. For higher vitamin content in tomatoes we go back to wild stock to improve what we have. That option remains open to us – provided wild tomatoes continue to exist.

Strawberries with cream are a treat for most people. But how did such tasty fruit originate? As far back as the 1600s strawberry plants discovered in Virginia, USA were brought back to France. Then a Captain Amédée-François Frézier discovered a new species in Chile that had large red fruit, far larger than the wild European strawberry. This too was brought back to France. The American and the Chilean species were successfully crossed to create new plants. These resulted in large sweet berries that saw the beginnings of modern commercial strawberry production which globally today is worth billions of dollars a year. But what if either of these wild species had become extinct before such a cross could be made? It is likely that we wouldn't even be aware of what we had lost.

So, if we want bigger flowers or finer plums or better disease resistance in corn we have an option to tap into existing wild stock. Indeed, we should never lose sight of the fact that everything we eat originated in the wild and that there are also innumberable other wild species out there. Could they possibly *all* be potentially useful?

At our present state of understanding most of them do not *appear* to display any obvious qualities of 'usefulness'. Are they therefore to be considered as having no value? Dangerous territory this. Should we, out of our stumbling guesswork, attempt to list those that might prove beneficial and focus our protection on these species, if necessary at the expense of the others? Dangerous and presumptuous territory indeed.

Brunel's Shield is used in tunnelling through soil. Since its invention it has saved hundreds of lives from tunnel collapses. This great engineer got his idea for such a shield from watching crickets tunnelling through mud. If crickets had become extinct before his time would Brunel have invented his shield? Before Brunel, would anyone have made an argument that crickets should be protected on the grounds that one day they might prove useful? We are told that spiders' webs, pound for pound, are stronger than steel cable. Perhaps one spider in particular might guide us towards the production of stronger and lighter cable than anything we now possess. But which species of spider? The structure of the exoskeleton of beetles or stick insects may, one day, stimulate us to invent a system that will allow some people to stand and to walk who would otherwise not be capable of doing either. But which species of stick insect, which beetle?

So, from a plainly selfish view, it is in our best interest that no species become extinct. Not a particularly noble and uplifting reason to conserve at all, but there it is. However, the problem with using the 'usefulness' argument is, I suspect, that many of us feel, in spite of the few examples offered above, that most species will turn out not to have any usefulness for us at all. And we might be right. But what is perceived today as having no conceivable value, may, a century from now, prove to hold the key to unlock wonderful inventions of extraordinary usefulness – that is, if in the meantime we don't drive these species to extinction. So there are big questions here that are fiendishly difficult to confront. The utilitarian argument for conservation may not be sufficiently strong to protect all species.

There is another argument, made by ecologists, for the protection of species. It is based on the view that the health of a habitat depends on the health of the constituent parts. Some will argue that the removal of a species from its ecological niche can bring about change, sometimes profound change, in the whole community. Some species are more critical than others in holding together whole complexities of plants and animals, for example grass or copepods or krill more than zebra or blackbirds, but I have never been comfortable with the view that the disappearance of some particular species from an ecosystem could unravel the entire mechanism. The disappearance of a particular tree in the Everglades would have drastic consequences for tree snails that depend exclusively on that one species, but would the entire system become unravelled with the disappearance of that particular species of tree?

I can see where the disappearance of the Florida alligator, whose strength is needed to dig water holes in times of drought, could affect the survival of dependent species, birds in particular. In this situation alligators are key; but in time things would adjust to the new circumstances and stabilize into a new set of arrangements.

If ecologists are to hold the confidence of the public, then they must never exaggerate the likely outcome of a situation when making their case. It is tempting to want to exaggerate beyond the known facts in order to win public support, especially when the opposition is shrill and often inaccurate in its counter-claims, but to do so is bad science. It also puts in jeopardy the trust of the public in accepting the views of scientists in other contentious and perhaps more important issues of conservation.

The loss of the familiar

We must be careful to make a distinction between what is a serious conservation issue and what is a concern but not a conservation matter. To exist at all we have to take from the enviroment what we need. We harvest plants and kill animals in order to eat. We cut timber that we may build shelters and other things we require. Whether we are devout Jainist monks or shrill conservationists we cannot remove ourselves from this reality. The First Nation peoples of North America recognised this dilemma. They showed respect for the animals they were compelled to kill. They told these animals that it was necessary for them to die in order that humans might live; however, humans, too, in time would die and their dust would fertilise the grass upon which young buffalo would graze and grow strong. It is a nice view – all things in time benefiting all things.

At one stage I worked for the British Columbia Forest Service. I was frequently taken aback at the scale of devastation a logging undertaking appeared to cause. What had been a fine forest of spruce and hemlock and cedar could quickly be turned into what some would see as a scarred landscape of stumps and twisted remains. An example of man at his worst? No, this is not mindless destruction. It is the harvesting of a crop of trees for the wood it contains to construct things that we need. Parasol ants strip leaves from trees to supply their needs. Locusts eat all before them. Gooseberry sawfly will leave a bush bare with nothing showing but twigs.

This apprehension about the destructive nature of logging might be put into context when measured against the harvesting of a field of corn. The visual results are no different.

The issue is merely one of scale. If we were at the size of mice our impression of the stubbles of a cornfield or a harvested field of cabbage would be the same. There would be stumps and twisted remains. Our reaction therefore at seeing a logged-out area is one primarily of aesthetics. We may experience considerable disturbance at the disappearance of a fine landscape, a landscape that can be replaced in time by new planting of trees. But we should not confuse this harvesting of timber, no matter how aesthetically crude the harvesting might be, with conservation issues. Certainly there would be justified concern if logging occurred in areas particularly rich in biodiversity or containing threatened species or was taking place in areas of 'old growth forest' where the trees have passed beyond the value of timber and into the realm of national totems. But we should not equate these justified conservation concerns with normal logging practices that are undertaken to harvest a needed resource. Tree growers might help alleviate some of the confusion here by referring to their holdings as 'tree farms' and not as 'forests' or 'woodlands', two words that imply a complexity of species living together in balance.

In this matter of logging, rather than expend our energy in fighting for a cause where no cause exists, we might insist on the establishment of tree farms, particularly in tropical regions. Such farms would reduce the pressures on natural forests and on the bewildering number of species to be found there.

In nature, on occasion, enormous destructive events occur. These unsettle us. A mountainside and all it contains might be swept away in a single night. We are left shocked that such a thing could happen. Part of the shock is the loss of the familiar. A single Douglas fir tree that each year unfailingly supports a pair of eagles becomes for us a place where we can be sure of seeing eagles. That dependability comforts us.

We may become particularly attached to a section of a stream that has a huge rock in its centre. It may be the place where we caught our first fish with our dad. It may be a place where we stopped awhile with our first girlfriend or our first boyfriend. These dependable and ever permanent features offer us anchorage in our own changing world. They become important for the assurance they give us that some things are constant, no matter what. We might have occasion to travel a far distance from home, and indeed stay away for years, but on our return, after we have met our family and played awhile with the family pet, we seek out that stream. And, yes, the big rock is still there, and further up the valley we can just about see the canopy of the eagle tree. Nothing has changed.

Some years ago a fine uncle of mine told me that an elderly lady was to visit Ireland from the USA. She had moved to America seventy years before and during all of that time had never once returned. Now she was anxious to see the small farm where she had been born. We located the farm and took the lady to places that were still important to her after all those years. One of the features she was anxious to find, and indeed we did find, was an ash tree on which she had carved her initials as a child. We cleaned the cloak of moss from the base of the tree, and there, to my silent and deep satisfaction, were the lady's initials still clearly discernable, if distorted, after years of that tree's growth. The discovery was one of the highlights of the lady's visit – permanency after seventy years of absence.

But events can occur – and all is swept away. If the big rock disappears and the very shape of the stream changes, and the huge ash tree crashes down and crumbles to dust, can anything at all be stable, can anything at all be trusted?

The Mount St. Helens eruption appalled us by the scale of what had occurred. A whole landscape, an entire mountain, a lake system changed utterly. The convulsions of that volcano forced American citizens, in particular, to confront the nature of our planet and the fragile contract we have to live here. The very shape of that mountain changed. The familiar disappeared. The new is everywhere. Nature has already moved back onto the grey slopes with her baskets of seeds, and, taking the changed circumstances on offer, settles new plants into the ash. Because this was a natural event, the shock, for most of us, heals over. We express awe and astonishment that such things happen. Then we adjust our thinking and move on with our lives.

But changes in the landscape, even small changes, brought about by what people do, can be more difficult to accept. We might deem such changes to be conservation issues worthy of protest, where in fact no such issues are involved.

An example might be a short stretch of road that for years had proven to be a bottleneck for traffic. Near my home, a number of years back, a case of this nature arose. The Roads Authorities decided that there was a need to widen the road at that section. The work would involve the removal of fifty trees. These trees were not particularly old nor were any of them rare. But we don't like change. We protest. We protest on grounds of conservation. Up until the news broke in the local newspaper we may not even have been aware of these fifty trees. Now they are about to be felled. We become incensed at such wanton destruction. It is strange, in this context, that our sensitivities were never disturbed by the hundreds of trees killed by pollution from the factory where we work. But now we are appalled at the pending destruction of these fifty trees. Independent environmental reports that concluded that the removal of these trees would have no harmful effect on the remaining forest do not dissuade us from holding our views. That the Roads Authorities will add an additional ten acres of land to the forest will not mollify us. We continue to be appalled. The question is why?

Our disposition may have nothing to do with the removal

of the fifty trees. It may be the case that we are disturbed, and have been for a considerable time, by a number of serious environmental issues that we had felt powerless to influence. We are dismayed when we read of the destruction of rainforests half a world away. We are angry when we hear about radioactive pollution in our seas, and of the holes punched through our protective ozone layer. We are made to feel helpless when confronting such destruction. We feel guilty too. Something should be done. Yet there is nothing practical that we, as individuals, appear to be able to do. Then we hear about the proposed removal of fifty trees in our locality. This is too much. Things have gone too far. We deflect our powerlessness and attempt to turn it into something positive. We will protest at the removal of our local trees. We will not stand by in the face of such mindless destruction. We will stand up and be counted. We shout our indignation into microphones. We give sound bytes of wisdom to any reporters who will listen. They take our photographs. For the first time in our lives we are noticed, we are famous – at least locally famous. That we have no particular qualifications in biology or ecology or forestry science does not stop us from dispensing our wisdom. We know nothing of the relationships of things within a forest environment. We know nothing of mycorrhiza or heart rot of trees. We know nothing of the turbulence of air currents moving across forest canopies. We know nothing of ring-shake or spiral growth patterns, nor do we know anything about fluting or root stability. We know nothing of the ecology of woodlands but we will express views on forestry matters to all who will listen.

This type of protest appears to be a relatively recent phenomenon. Such misguided protests can have real cost implications. The proposed road improvement scheme was repeatedly deferred, and as a result the cost rose by several million euro before the road widening was completed.

With increasing frequency such emotional surges can do

great harm to serious conservation issues where strong public strength of feeling would be invaluable. Engaging in pseudo-environmental circuses weakens the impact of real public demonstration when it is truly needed. If we are to take part in public displays we should choose our battlegrounds carefully and only take part in protestations that have *real* conservation issues at their heart.

The adventure of existence itself

Many species now extinct were beautiful creatures once with wonderful names that stirred our imagination – the giant flightless owls of Cuba or the laughing owls of New Zealand; the Samoan wood rail; the pygmy hippopotamus and the legendary dodo. The songs and sounds of these delightful things are now lost to us.

In Ireland we once had a fine bird of the reedbeds – the bittern. When I was young the call of this bird could be heard on a still night booming along the Shannon River, the longest river in the country. This haunting sound of the male bird proclaiming his territory could be heard five kilometres away. The strangeness of the call made the hairs on one's neck stand on end. But now, at evening time, we can stand on the bank of that great river – and there is silence. We are the poorer in that.

Today, across the world, wonderful birds and animals are close to their tipping point. Are they, like the Cuban yellow bats, to become for us a receding memory of creatures that once were? If they do slip away they will leave behind them a less interesting world.

We need to sweep away a number of illusions. If we are to become effective in conservation we must first stop deluding ourselves: we are not winning the battle for conservation. Government agencies create nature reserves, sanctuaries, national parks, biosphere reserves and other similar undertakings to protect wildlife. We develop national and international laws to protect endangered species. We put in place agencies to fight illegal trafficking in species and species' products; yet with all of that in place we are still not winning the battle. True, we can point to a number of skirmishes that we have won, or appear to have won. The whooping crane project, the Arabian oryx undertaking, the work to protect the nana goose, and in my own country the protection of the peregrine falcon and the introduction of the golden eagle that had been extinct there for almost a hundred years. But these successes are only campaigns. The real battle is not for swamplands; it is not for Indian rhino, it is not even for ozone. If conservation is to succeed the battle must be for the minds of people.

All of us can produce figures on the scale of the disappearance of species. We can argue the magnitude of such figures. We can argue the reasons why. But we cannot argue against the fact that many wild species are now finding it impossible to share this planet with us.

No country, no statesman, no philosopher, no ecologist has all the answers to this problem. We need to acknowledge that all of us, to varying degrees, contribute to the damage that is done. We fuddle along, wishing that things would be different, and yet none of us have clean hands in any of this. We may not pollute directly – leaving that to others in the manufacture of stuff that we buy. In this situation what we don't need are strident voices reminding us of this at every opportunity. We don't need accusations that ratchet up our guilt. What we *do* need is some process to lift us out of the seeming inevitability of it all.

Scientists cannot solve conservation problems. Restorative ecology may be resorted to if things go badly wrong. The ecologist will come bearing bandages and liniments to patch up the damage we have caused. But the conditions that trigger the problem in the first place they will not be able to treat. Those reside within us, in our lack of a vibrant ethic towards wild things.

Many years ago I remember reading a headline in the *St Petersburg Times* in Florida, 'To hell with conservation, I want my job.' And when we are honest with ourselves, that is where most of us live our lives in our attitude to conservation.

In Aldo Leopold's book *A Sand Country Almanac* there appears a statement that is as relevant today as it was when it first made its appearance in 1949: *There is as yet no social stigma in the possession of a gullied farm, a wrecked forest, or a polluted stream, provided the dividends suffice to send the youngsters to college.*

What has brought us to this? Indeed, was there ever a time when attitudes were different? If Bronze Age people had been given powerful tractors and chain saws and agricultural chemicals, would they have behaved differently? The answer is we don't know. But when we attempt to compare our thinking with the thinking of those who have gone before us there does seem to be one significant difference. Our ancestors appear to have been acutely alive to the presence of the environment that pressed in about them on every side. They appear to have been keenly aware of their dependence on that environment for their survival. They were attentive to the movement of buffalo and whales and gazelle. They were watchful for the return of salmon and of the movement of geese overhead. In some years they became uneasy at the lack of rain. They became afraid at the sun's apparent reluctance to rise in the depths of winter. They studied the hunting adroitness of wolf packs and lions. They watched the shadow movements of leopards in trees. They recognized their gods in the wind. They recognized them in the rumbles of black clouds. All of this was as natural to them as their skin. As a consequence they held the land and all it contained sacred and treated it with respect.

We, today, are largely uncoupled from any sense of dependency on land. In Europe and America this detachment seems to have become particularly so since the late 1940s. Our confidence in what we could achieve was running high back then. Science, engineering and petrochemicals would solve all problems. We would take three tons of food from soil where before only one was possible. We would divert rivers to irrigate millions of acres. We would sweep aside hedges and drain what was wet. What had been a hundred small fields became a single unit of wheat. We no longer had need for the rainmaker's songs. The press of a button would be all it would take to mist a field until the crop ran with water. Those things that had once been familiar to us – things that had lived and flitted about in our hedgerows – were thrown back and forced to make do with the few boundary ditches that separated one farm from the next. Soon we began to lose understanding of those things; then we ceased to notice them at all; in time, some of us even forgot their names.

In our march towards efficiency we pushed nature to one side. We lost contact with what had once been familiar. In detaching ourselves we lost something of value: we lost the assurance of our place in the mix of it all. We are the poorer by that detachment. We need to find our way back to our place.

Out of its own magnificence nature can speak to us more eloquently than any clamorous voice raised on her behalf. Quietly falling snow or the music of geese speak of beauty that should be cherished. So our way back towards nature should begin quietly, each person taking it at his or her own pace, each meeting nature in their own way in small things. Our journey should begin with the observation of the small. It begins when we allow ourselves time to see what is not observed in a rush, how wind combs a ripe cornfield – such a simple thing to do but not unimportant for all that.

Our way back begins when we start to notice the oriental eyes of wild hares among grass, when we take time to watch the nervous flight of sand martins before thunder or the low swoop of swallows before rain. Observing wildlife in its uncomplicated simplicity will help us journey back to the certainty that nature has to offer us.

We have one particular quality that should help us in this journey – our ability to wonder. It is intriguing to speculate whether we alone have this capacity. I had an old bearded collie as a house pet. Alas she died fifteen months ago. During her life I saw her many times sit in the sunlight in what appeared to be contentment beyond mere living. Several times I put the question to her if she had ever felt wonderment. Wise dog that she was, she always refused to answer, and settled for a good scratch from a human who doesn't know very much. Left with the silence of a fine dog on the matter, I have to assume that humans, and only humans, have this ability to be fascinated. It is this capacity that may help us take our first shadowy steps towards a conservation ethic.

This ability to reflect is a powerful advantage in helping us to find our way back. Whales and condors do impress us, and we respond with a lurching reaction that something should be done to save such fine creatures. If we believe in the evolution of things, then all are related – howler monkeys, tree snails and man. We are simply different parts of the great adventure of existence itself. There should, therefore, be no room for discussion on the 'usefulness' or on the 'beauty' of any species. All are family. All are beautiful. It is from this position that conservation should flow.

Economic arguments on the importance of gene banks, good though such claims may be, are not the basis on which we can hope to persuade society to adopt a more responsible attitude in its dealings with nature. Such arguments in the end would not protect the broad and deep roar of most of creation. Better that we view *all* life as beautiful and part of a very ancient song. When each of us can hear that song then the true cost of things, and the freedom that we now give to industry to produce products on our behalf, will be evaluated in a new light.

There are few Mahatma Gandhis in the world. Where we lack statesmen we have politicians. The political life of those who would represent us depends on one particular skill: that he or she is accurately tuned into the real thinking of their voting public. If voters are indifferent to conservation why should we expect a politician to become unduly exercised in the matter? Politicians dare not lead where their voters do not want to go – the consequences at election time would be disastrous.

So, rather than criticize our politicians we should understand that if they are to do something for us, we must first give them our help. They need clear signals that conservation matters, and they need those signals coming at them in numbers. With that authority in hand they can act effectively on our behalf. They can walk the same road as their voters and do what is possible because they have the comfort of the assurances of those they would lead.

All of us periodically need to meet life afresh and embrace it anew. We need once again to embrace nature in her exuberance and vitality. We need to acknowledge her unknowable mystery and know that we are her children. Most important of all we must discover anew that we too are part of nature and not set apart from her. We must return again to the realization that men and women, with their baskets of needs and dreams and ambitions, are part of this great stream of life.

How can we ever hope to be concerned for nature if we fail to recognise that hummingbirds and small boys dance under the same sunlight? If we fail to make that connection then we will fail in our ambitions for conservation. We need, therefore, to form a closer relationship with nature.

And how might we do that?

Remembering Encounters with Nature

The Giving of a Nature Name

> *When a Sioux Indian would take the calumet, the pipe, he would hold it up, stem to the sky, so that the sun could take the first puff. And then he'd address the four directions always. In that frame of mind, when you're addressing yourself to the horizon, to the world that you're in, then you're in your place in the world. It's a different way to live.*[1]

I have on a bookshelf above my desk a small postcard that gives meaning to the Christian name of my youngest child. This card says a little about the origin of the name 'Philip'. Among a number of other things the card tells me that this name stems from the Greek 'Philippos', meaning 'Lover of Horses'. My son has a passion for sailing but I have not known him to display any particular interest in horses. But there it is.

Some years before Philip was born I spent five pleasant months living in a First Nation village in British Columbia, Canada. Coming from an island off the mainland of Europe where people are keenly conscious of family or clan names, I was intrigued to learn of a different kinship in use by these Canadian people. Some of them were 'Beaver' people; others were 'Fireweed' people and so on. When a chief of the Beaver people died they placed on his grave a statue of a beaver. That image has stayed with me down the years.

It's a comforting thing to know one's family origins or one's clan name. It gives us the security of a place in the continuum of a fraternity of people. These labels, however, do not carry an echo of nature about them, or if they do we may often not recognize them for that, as we can in the case of the Beaver people many miles north of Vancouver in British Columbia, or the Fireweed people. Before clans were, before names were, we were people of nature. Indeed back then our survival depended on – and still depends on – the natural processes that drive this planet. We were once keenly aware of that – now we are less so. Whether in fear or awe or wonder we lived our lives with the constancy of nature about us on all sides. It was there in the clamour of broad-winged swans overhead urging us to attend to the woodpile for the gathering winter. It was there in the first trickle of bright water from ice sheets that told us that the cold season was once again on the wane. It was there in the eager joy of swans once more in the sky, this time in their urgent need that young of their kind might be born. We had no need then of calendars to metronome the seasons. The nesting of crows, the quickening of green corn, red apples falling soundlessly into long grass were enough back then.

But somewhere along the way we became modern. It's not that we simply moved to cities to give our lives to VDU screens. Many who still work the land today have also severed their ancient connections. We now farm from dust-proof cabins bolted onto powerful tractors. In such air-conditioned 'rooms' we listen to the latest weather information and the fluctuations in the price of grain and the sounds of country music. We turn our great ploughs along the headlands to set the lines once more towards thin hedgerows in the distance. Our grandfathers, when ploughing, walked behind horses and took an understanding of their land through the vibrations of the plough handles. They knew where the soft patches lay and where the tongues of grit fanned out from rocky headlands. But to a man high up on a tractor, grit and soft are all the same to be ploughed through and under. Even the gravel-squawks of rooks dancing on the chocolate-coloured ribbons behind the great ploughs are no longer in the ears of tractor drivers sealed in their cabins of isolation. There is something else too. Where once farmers worked their land with a sense of what was right by nature, now we pay grants that they do the same. There is something awfully skewed in all of this.

We have shunted ourselves into a condition where most of us are largely indifferent to nature. We are not anti-nature; that would be going a step too far. Indeed it saddens us to read of the disappearance of a species or of the destruction of a piece of rainforest. These are genuine concerns. They may be genuine but they don't register at an intensity that we demand change. Part of the reason is that we lead far too busy lives. Should it be any surprise therefore that we have little time to be concerned about nature? We have hardly time for ourselves. We soothe our misgivings about our inaction by a simple rationale. Governments are responsible for the protection of nature. Governments create national parks. They set aside land as nature reserves. They do this on our behalf. A bit of comfort in that. Only a small step then to slip down into the comforting view that nature conservation is not our responsibility – we pay taxes and leave it to others. This thinking is lopsided. We are left without any feelings of obligation or accountability for conservation.

If nature is to be accommodated we need to move back from this position of paralysis. We need to re-establish a kinship with the wildlife that surrounds us. We need to rediscover the beauty and the dignity we can find there. Against the odds, on the edge of a busy street, a solitary dandelion might push up between slabs of concrete. She might produce a single yellow flower, the best flower she can grow.

We pass her simple display without a glance. She makes the route along which we travel that much softer by her single green rosette of leaves and her glowing yellow flower. Yet, for all that, we do not even see her, do not appreciate the best that she can offer us. Sharing the rain and dust and smog of our cities these unassuming plants give us their flowers and their optimism – and we pass them by without noticing them.

I'd like to return now to that small card with the words 'Philip – Lover of Horses'. What has this got to do with the process of edging our way back towards nature? In one way a lot. We can accumulate riches and gather in about us high acclaim and yet experience hollowness at the centre of it all. Without the realization that we are part of something deep and vast and very ancient we feel incomplete, as a child might be when momentarily separated from its mother. If we are to be content there is a need to re-establish our contact with this ancient home.

The First Nation peoples of North America commonly gave themselves, or had bestowed upon them by others, names that associated them with elements of nature:

> Liwanu (Miwok) – 'growl of a bear'
> Telutci (Miwok) – 'a bear making dust'
> Tolinka (Miwok) – 'flapping ear of a coyote'
> Wauna (Miwok) – 'singing snow goose'
> Huata (Miwok) – 'carrying seeds in a basket'
> Hesutu (Miwok) – 'yellow jacket nest rising out of the ground'
> Kuwanyamtiwa (Hopi) – 'beautiful badger going over the hill'
> Nova (Hopi) – 'chases butterfly'
> Honiahaka (Cheyenne) – 'little wolf'
> Nastas (Navajo) – 'curve-like foxtail grass'
> Tecumseh (Shawnee) – 'panther passing across'

At birth some Aboriginal children in Australia are given the name of an animal or plant. Throughout their lives they will then treat this animal or plant as particularly special to them.

A 'frog person' might stop his or her car and remove a frog from the road and place it out of harm's way. A small act perhaps when seen in isolation, but frogs have something good going for them if such kindness is repeated by many. Because of their names, individuals will make sure that such animals or plants are not hurt or damaged. We can learn something valuable from this.

There is a wonderful custom among some of the Karen people of Burma. When a child is born the father carries the placenta into the forest. He offers the afterbirth of his child to a tree. He does this by placing it on a branch or burying it at the base of the tree. When the newborn grows into some years the father brings the child to the forest to see his or her 'life tree'. From then on, to that child, this tree is special; it marks the day when the child came into the world. And later on, that particular tree will continue to be special to the child and will not be endangered in any way, and, by extension, the whole forest where that tree grows becomes of great importance to that person. That way lies conservation; that way is the beginning of an ethic to conserve things. Here there is no need for lectures. Why? Because he or she has had a direct contact with something in nature that is meaningful in a personal way.[2]

In all of these instances there is an important lesson for us. Such examples hold out opportunities to help us find our way back towards nature. So we might consider the following.

We give names to our children to identify who they are. There is no reason why we could not also bestow on each child a 'nature name'. Such a name need not be given at the time of birth. Indeed it might be best if it were not given until some incident occurs that links that child in a particular way with some event of nature, for example, when the child, while playing in the snow, finds a wren more dead than alive and carries it indoors and two days later releases it fully recovered. This small event would be a significant moment for the child. To commemorate it, the child might be given the name 'Wren in out of the storm', which would define the bird and the circumstance that had brought the child and bird together. Such a name would catch the understanding conveyed in the names used by the First Nation peoples or could even be translated into one of their beautiful euphonic names.

Depending on the particular circumstances, other names might be 'Snow geese coming down', 'Cranes overhead', 'Bear at my window', 'Leopard among trees', etc. When the child is old enough the parents should explain the circumstance that brought about his or her particular nature name and that from then on that particular animal or plant should be special to it.

In conferring nature names on children it would be important that the names are not contrived. Neither should a 'suitable' name be thought up by a doting parent, nor should a parent place a child in a situation out of which a 'suitable' name might be arrived at. Nature names should occur spontaneously out of an unexpected event and not simply be the name of an animal or plant and no more. So 'Butterfly' or 'Willow Tree' or 'Little Egret' or 'Sea Otter' would not be sufficient. And once a name is picked it should not be replaced at a later date if a 'bigger' or 'better' event occurs.

I remember once as a six-year old my mother bringing me to the seaside and settling me down on a blanket. It was one of those rare, warm, sunny days in August in Ireland. In a half drowse I lay in the delicious heat listening to the waves turn and turn about, breaking on the shore, rushing forward then drawing back again with a hissing sound stitched through with the cry of oystercatchers further along the beach. Then there was a pitter-patter of things falling all about us. I sat up on the rug. Hundreds of red ladybird beetles were dropping out of the sky and settling on me, my mother, the blanket and the sand dunes around us. Yet still more fell, and folding their delicate tracery wings under the protective dome of their backs they walked on the dry grass blades and on the rug and on the hamper basket. Why this demonstration of ladybird power occurred is a mystery to me. It has never happened since, nor do I know anyone who has had a similar experience. This was a small incident where nature unexpectedly forced its way into the otherwise quiet, sleepy life of a six-year old on a beautiful summer's afternoon – an experience to be captured in a nature name! Such a simple thing to do, and it costs nothing.

Fine, but how can this giving of a nature name help in the conservation of nature? Well, for a start it is not possible for any of us to bring all of nature into our understanding. It is simply too vast and too complex to make sense of it all. Better, then, that each one of us tries to understand just a tiny piece of it. To most of us the cloud of complexity that envelops the word 'habitat' or the word 'environment' is overwhelming. The protection of habitats is key to conservation, yet 'habitat' is just too big a concept to fathom. But one species? Yes, I reckon I could grow to understand a lot of things about one species – and from out of this I will begin to understand something about the habitat in which it lives.

By understanding a little about the animal or plant in our nature name we can begin to comprehend how that particular plant or animal fits into the larger picture. We see more clearly the associations between that plant, or animal, and the things around it. We begin to see that it does not exist in isolation from its surroundings, and that if we damage the surroundings in which that animal or plant lives we threaten its survival. In the end we come to realise that all are connected and each is an integral part of the whole. At this point we begin to get a glimmer of the interconnectedness of everything and of our place in the fit of it all. And it starts with learning as much as possible about the animal or plant in our nature name.

This jolt to our senses of how we are all connected is the beginning of our journey towards a responsible conservation ethic. What is right for nature can now begin to grow within us and become a position from which we make judgements on issues that affect wildlife. If parents are prepared to bestow 'nature names' on their children then we have a mechanism to guide our young towards a stronger link to nature and to further their awareness of belonging to a living complex system. This security in belonging will carry contentment into adulthood. Nature too will benefit. Parents willing to run with this simple idea could be part of a world movement to improve matters for wildlife.

At this stage it is necessary to raise the word 'cynicism'. We are surrounded by cynics. Some will make it their business to pronounce that the idea of 'nature names' is silly and unworkable. I can only hope that parents, by embracing this simple idea, will prove them wrong. As things now stand we are losing species to extinction. If the cynics can do something about that it would be most useful, and most welcome, because it will take all of us working together to improve things for conservation. Governments can only do so much. What is not in place at the moment is a sustained public concern for conservation. A feeling of *right by nature* should be part of our thinking without the need to be a member of a club or organisation. The giving of nature names to our children is a practical step to bringing this about.

Some parents may initially feel foolish about giving their children 'nature names'. At the start of this potential world movement, when few will have given such names to their children, this is understandable. But as more people warm to the idea it will begin to become a good thing to do; and finally it will become the most natural thing in the world. If we are not to continue losing species on a world level we must attempt something new. 'Nature names' would make a difference. They would become part of the process of putting in place a world environmental ethic.

An ethic is not a mysterious piece of thinking. It is simply a feeling of what is the right thing to do under a set of circumstances. Why would someone purposely swerve their car in order to hit a rabbit or a badger?

When I was a student I worked for a time as a bus conductor in London. One particular driver, on the early shift starting at 5.30 in the morning, would slowly prowl round a corner in his double-decker bus looking for pigeons feeding in the road. Very carefully he would creep up with his bus until the moment was right. Then he would put his foot to the floor and on a good day kill two or three pigeons. There is something badly wrong with this mind-set. The animal or bird becomes a 'thing' in the headlights. It is not seen for its perfection, for what it is to be a rabbit or a badger or a pigeon. In similar manner a butterfly flapping against a closed window will die of dehydration. By opening the window and releasing her you free her of her dilemma. It does something else too. It frees up something in the person who helped her out. So the gesture is repaid in equal measure. A simple thing like this can be the beginning of a conservation ethic. Practical conservation in your vicinity is more beneficial than worrying about the loss of habitat on the other side of the planet. The growth of a conservation ethic starts with small adjustments. The bestowing of nature names can be that first step.

In time, this practice can become widespread. Children, on growing up and talking to others, will discover that they have the name of the same animal or plant embedded in their particular 'nature name'. The circumstances of how they acquired their name may be different, but similarly named people might want to form loose associations of 'Badger people' or 'Willow people' or 'Wolf people' or 'Tiger people' or 'Wren people', and so on. It is only a small step then that such like-named people would want to band together as one voice should their particular animal or plant come under threat in any part of the world. What if within a country, through the wonders of the internet, the 'Owl people' sought out each other to form an association that would speak for owls where owl habitats are endangered? The 'Badger people' or the 'Wolf people' or the 'Frog people' or the 'Anteater people' or the 'Hummingbird people' could also form associations to speak for their particular species where threats arise.

There is authority in numbers; there is political power in numbers. We might, therefore, take this idea further. What if associations for a particular species or genus were to form a *worldwide* political lobby? We could have a world federation of 'Wolf people' who might voice their concern if wolves in any part of the world were to come under particular pressure. Likewise we could have 'Butterfly people' or 'Sandhill Crane people' or 'Cactus people' who would speak out of their collective authority against any issues in any part of the world that would threaten the habitats of the species or genus they represent.

We might take this further still. Where a habitat that contains several species of interest to different groups comes under threat, might not these groups band together to form a bigger pressure group to protect that particular habitat? Often conservation concerns are registered in too wide a net, attempting to conserve everything. Conservationists in such a situation can be seen as being unrealistic, as not being practical. Far better, then, that they focus only on one or two species when registering their concerns. This will be seen as far less a diffuse argument, as far more reasonable in its ambition. And if the habitat is finally saved in this way, it is also saved for all the other species which depend on that piece of ground.

Conservationists should consider this approach as a strategy. All of this is possible, but it starts by giving nature names to our children. This simple commitment could, in time, grow into a worldwide movement for nature conservation. Those, therefore, who profess an affinity for nature should consider this proposal.

1. Joseph Campbell, with Bill Moyers: *The Power of Myth* (Doubleday, 1988), p. 92.
2. *See* 'The Winds of Change: Karen People in Harmony with World Heritage' by Seri Thongmak and David L. Hulse, in *The Law of the Mother – Protecting Indigenous People in Protected Areas*, edited by Elizabeth Kemf, Sierra Club Books, San Francisco, 1993, pp. 162-8.

> *A World Event for Nature*

The Children-of-the-World Nature Reserve

Wouldn't it be wonderful if children were to donate dollars and pounds and euro and pennies and cents and yen and ringgits and cruzeiros and other small change from the currencies of the world? What if all of this money came together with the imprint of children's hands on it?

What if it came together to make a big pool of value! Japanese money that had travelled to Okayama out of the valleys in the Chugoku Sanchi; money collected in the humid towns of Manicoré and Humaita and put into tiny boats which go down the Madeira before hitting the great wash of the Amazon River itself; dollars and cents with the smell of wealth about them from the towering cities of Los Angeles, Miami and Boston; coins too from Irkutsk and Magadan and Tomsk; coins from the rich children of Sweden and some from the poor children of Sweden; English coins from the hands of children that had petted small cats, and from Saudi Arabia, Bahrain and Qatar little coins and some big coins that had specks of sand on them, because they are coins of the desert.

Every country would assemble the donations of its children into one heap. Fat countries would give quite a lot. That would be all right. Countries not so fat would make fewer donations. That would be fine too. A number of thin countries would give little. Their contributions would be appreciated most of all.

From the figures of the US Census Bureau 2002 it was projected that the number of children between 0 and 14 years of age by the year 2010 would be about 1.8 billion. If one in a hundred children, say between the ages of 5 and 14 years, made a donation, then we would be looking at quite a few million contributions from children. All of these generous gifts from the children of the world would create a possibility. A possibility to do what? It would have to be something that children would be inspired by, that would be great for children to do. Something that would allow them to say years later, "I was part of that."

We could bring bags of coins – representing all the donations collected from children from around the world – to the United Nations Building in New York. We could organise a 'Ceremony of Giving'. Small children from many nations would take cupped hands of coins and give them up into the safe hands of the Secretary General of the United Nations. The Secretary General would accept the coins from each child, and, symbolically, the entire amount from the children of the world. Then the Secretary General would announce that the money would be used for the creation of the very first 'Children-of-the-World Nature Reserve'.

Those to be entrusted with the establishment of the reserve would then be presented with the moneys to do so, and the location of the reserve would be announced. The reserve would be in an area that is politically stable, free from major diseases and easily accessible. If it is to be beneficial to nature and hold the imagination of small children, the reserve should be rich in biodiversity. It might be part of a tropical rainforest, a swampland rich in wildlife, an island or a section of a coral reef. Wherever it might be, it will be special to the children who made it possible.

Park staff would manage the reserve on behalf of the children. They might build a village there, so that some children could visit. Wildlife rangers would show them what they had helped to create and what they were helping to protect. For the children who could not visit, the reserve would engage in outreach programmes. A newsletter would travel through websites to keep children around the world informed about events in *their* reserve. They might be shown hatching turtles, or the power of a monsoon that had destroyed a whole section of forest. They might hear of a new discovery – a species of snail or dragonfly until then unknown to science. They might be shown butterflies that had never been seen before.

Nature reserves have running costs. Part of the money collected from children would be set aside for this need. On leaving childhood, ownership of the reserve would pass to the next generation of children and they would become the custodians of the reserve. Every ten years children across the world would be asked anew for donations to maintain their reserve. In this change of ownership from one generation of children to the next, one thing would remain: samples of coins from the children who initially made it all possible would be on permanent display in the reserve.

We can do this. We can organise for children to donate money towards the creation of such a reserve. We can then bring the reserve into existence on behalf of the children and manage it on their behalf.

We should have no illusions about the degree of organisation needed to make all of this happen. But a considerable advantage in bringing a nature reserve into existence in this fashion will be the publicity it will generate. This, in turn, would bring into focus the difficulty wildlife is now experiencing. That our children or grandchildren are attempting to do something for nature would make us pause and reflect on our own attitudes to conservation.

Publicity will be everything if we are to generate excitement for the project. We will need to collect the equivalent of many millions of dollars. Collecting such a large amount of money in this fashion and from children will galvanize public curiosity and enthusiasm for what is proposed. High profile statesmen and celebrities will be invited to be associated with the project to further heighten publicity. There is another consideration. This Alice-in-Wonderland way of collecting money will appeal enormously to children. This will be especially so when it is explained to them that other children from all around the world will also be taking part in the venture.

The high point of all of this publicity will be when the final tally of money is revealed on the steps of the UN Building. That small children from many nationalities will be present will add to the emotional content of the occasion. The event would be seen as the beginning of an undertaking where children would start to become part of the process of wildlife conservation. That is why, with all its lumbering awkwardness, we should go this way in collecting donations from children.

Publicity is the most costly thing to purchase. There will be a thousand stories of how donations were collected and brought from remote places and how they were stored and guarded along the route before reaching their final destination. The media would track the progress as money is accumulated into bigger heaps, first at county or district level and finally at country level. The publicity will snowball the project forward so that it gathers momentum and generates its own success.

Running in tandem with the fund-raising project will of course be the search for the area where the reserve might be established. Experienced park managers and ecologists (semi-tropical and tropical systems) would be required to identify important sites. Discussions would need to take place with several heads of states to seek agreement on the conditions under which a reserve might be established.

Many people from many countries will need to get involved. Sometimes it will be fun, but there will be frustration in good measure too. We will confront bureaucracy. We will confront inertia and indifference. But, in addition, we will come in contact with wonderful people who will want to help in surprising ways. I have no doubt about that. Also there will be misunderstandings and cultural shock – and sometimes meanness. There will be kindness from unexpected quarters, and sometimes despair whether we will ever succeed in what we are attempting to do. But deep personal satisfaction will be drawn from an event that has changed our approach to the conservation of wildlife.

Broad practical steps will need to be put in place to make this project a success. A steering committee would have to be assembled. This committee would critically examine the proposal and widen it out in detail. Above all it would need to agree practical lines of approach to create what is intended. Of great importance would be solid management experience on how best to guide a project of this nature and scale. In addition there would need to be an agreed time frame for different stages of the project.

As a first stage, the committee would produce a draft document which would then have to be circulated to others, in particular to key conservation organisations for their comments. Following from this, two working documents would be prepared. One would set out the methodology on how best to organize the collecting of donations from children. Conditions of course will vary from country to country. Some countries do not allow their children to have money; children from a number of countries will have nothing to give. Individual countries which take part in the project will be expected to modify what is suggested to accomodate their own particular circumstances. The second document would establish the criteria to be adopted in selecting a site suitable for their type of reserve. It would also offer guidance on how discussions for such lands might take place. Political and diplomatic skills will be needed in negotiating the purchase or lease of a potentially favourable site.

There will be costs incurred to set up and organise the project. No money collected from children should be used for this purpose. Sponsorship from a selected number of global corporations or from wealthy philanthropic individuals will be sought to cover these costs. None of this sponsored money will be channelled towards the creation of the reserve itself. This must be achieved through the efforts of the children. All funds donated by children must be spent on the acquisition, or leasing, of the site, the putting in place of the necessary infrastructures and the running costs of the reserve itself. Matching funds to equal those donated by the children will be sought from the United Nations.

Co-ordinating the collecting of contributions from children is important. Each participating country will need to put in place its own local steering committee to oversee this part of the project. School structures, where they exist, might prove to be the best mechanism for reaching large numbers of children. Spirited backing by governments will be essential if we are to go this route. For this to happen the project will need to have on board at least one or two highly influential politicians or ex-politicians who would be prepared to pick up the telephone and put calls through to various heads of state to win their backing for what is intended.

Even with that in place, a flow of information on the nature and purpose of the project will be needed to motivate teachers, parents and, in particular, the children themselves. Children's television programmes will be critical factors in explaining what is intended and how children can help. A 'Musical Concert for Nature' might be considered – to give wide publicity to the project.

In organizing the collection of donations it will be important that we are aware of regional customs and practices, so that no misunderstandings arise. In most countries nothing less than full approval of the ruling head or president will be required. Some countries will be closed to the idea no matter what approaches are made. We need to accept this, move on, and work to involve as many countries as is practical.

These are the broad outlines for what is intended. The details will reveal themselves through committee meetings and the advice of many. The first step is to put in place a steering committee to take charge of this project to create the first 'Children-of-the-World Nature Reserve.

> **An Appeal to the Religious Leaders of the World**

The Quest through Togetherness

The Creation of a World Wilderness Reserve by the Great Religions of the World

> *Spirit ancestors created the landscape. Aborigines believe that part of the creator stays with each piece of the landscape. It is for this reason that all land is sacred to Aboriginal people.*[1]

Today – how far we have moved from that belief! It is an astonishing fact that there is a broad road towards nature that has surprisingly few footprints upon it. All religions affirm the presence of a Deity – or a multiplicity of deities – who reigns over all. The universe and all it contains is one expression of the existence of this Presence. Many of the great religions see in this beauty and in this complexity of nature a manifestation of the presence of He Who Is. Surely this is a basis for religious organisations to take leadership roles in the protection of nature?

Nature is in deep trouble and needs their help. World religious leaders could play a tremendous part in conservation. Hundreds of millions of their followers would listen to what they would say. At present there is little evidence of religious organisations offering guidance on the need to accommodate wildlife. Surely such organisations could guide their followers towards a wildlife conservation ethic? On one day of each year religious leaders could speak in their temples or mosques or churches of how their congregations might help in the protection of species. One day a year! A letter of instruction is all it would take. In this simple way religions could be part of a conservation movement that would speak out for the great whales and for turtles and for butterflies.

If nature indeed is an expression of the work of a Supreme Being, it seems puzzling that religions are largely silent on conservation matters. In the past some religious thinkers have argued that nothing is important in this life, that we should not reflect on the beauty around us, that this world is no more than a preparation for what lies beyond. These are disheartening views when we look at the wonders that lie around us on every side. This is even more puzzling when we consider that many of the great religious founders felt it necessary to seek out wilderness areas to draw closer to their God. Mohammed left his home in Mecca to go to a mountain cave to meditate. The Buddha went into solitude and sitting beneath a bo tree received the illumination he was seeking. Jesus, Son of God of the Christian Faith, retired to the desert that he too might meditate.

There appears to be a quality in wilderness that allows great spiritual minds to discover what they seek. Some, on going to such places, enter into deep contemplation and find their God in the quietness of falling snow and in the fingering of the wind among leaves. If wilderness does indeed have such qualities then surely religious leaders should be anxious that there will always be wild places? For many of us less spiritual, these beautiful places can stop us in our tracks and compel us to reflect on a mystery inexpressibly greater than that which lies before us. Such qualities of wild lands are worth preserving.

A tall forest of cedars can be a good place to be in at four o'clock in the afternoon. I was in northern British Columbia, two day's walk from the nearest road. The trees were five centuries old; there was thick moss on the ground, and stillness. Crossing a river I came upon an animal track that slipped off among the trees. Not a sound could be heard in all of that great forest. Ancient cedars seem to hold about them a stillness that is akin to the silence of fog. Then he appeared – a timber wolf, ghostwalker of the woods. So silently had he trickled over the trail that not the slightest sound betrayed his coming. Perhaps he had not come at all. Perhaps he had materialized before me – as though such things were possible in a cedar forest. The wolf stopped. He stared at me out of oriental eyes. He was not afraid, nor did he show aggression. We were equal, the timber wolf and I. Both knew it. Both delighted in the knowing. The eyes of the wolf, half lost in the grizzled mist that cloaked his head, were not from the world of storybooks. Eyes and fur and stance were out of a time of wilderness before men were.

Standing in the quietness among those ancient cedars I longed to know that wolf. I wanted to pass through the silence that separates one species from another. I wanted to go down on my knees and wrap an arm about his neck. I wanted that we could spend a little time together, that we could play together – and share something that neither could express; something more important than men, something even more important than wolves.

But we did not play among the cedars. The wolf, having given a few moments of his existence to a creature who did not know many things, turned away and continued ghost-walking through the forest at four o'clock in the afternoon. I walked for some distance along the spidery trail – but the wolf had gone as enigmatically as he had come.

This momentary appearance of the wolf, with sunlight slanting down through tall trees, gave me a moment of reflection on the mystery of that forest. A forest that lacks ghostwalkers is a pale thing indeed. So I offer the following: as wilderness areas are under threat, wildlife would benefit from the creation of a World Religious Wilderness Reserve.

The great religions, it would appear, are not entirely comfortable with each other. Part of this is due to past circumstances. Part of it is due to the certainty that each is the true way towards the Supreme Being. Part of it is due to the unspoken competition to harvest additional souls into their separate boats. And there is something else too – a sense of strangeness; the strangeness of each other's rituals and beliefs; even the strangeness of each other's clothing and food.

Are religions forever to remain at a distance from each other? Do they not all worship the same unknowable Entity, be it in different ways? Are not all following the true way but only doing so along different paths? If strangeness between those who worship in different ways is ever to be eliminated it must start with clerics meeting together in relaxed circumstances – and where better than in a place of striking beauty that is a manifestation of the hand of God!

A world wilderness reserve would be financed, managed and collectively owned by the great religions of the world. Clearly such a protected area, chosen for its richness in biodiversity, would benefit the animals and plants within its boundaries – a place of high mountains and towering rocks, of water and open sky, of scree slopes, alpine meadows and snow, and a place of silence where spiritual people can draw closer to their God or gods. Development within such a reserve would be restricted to the simple needs of those who would visit it.

All the great religions – each according to their means and with an open generosity of full co-operation – would contribute to the cost of establishing such a protected wilderness area. I can only offer the bare bones of this idea here.

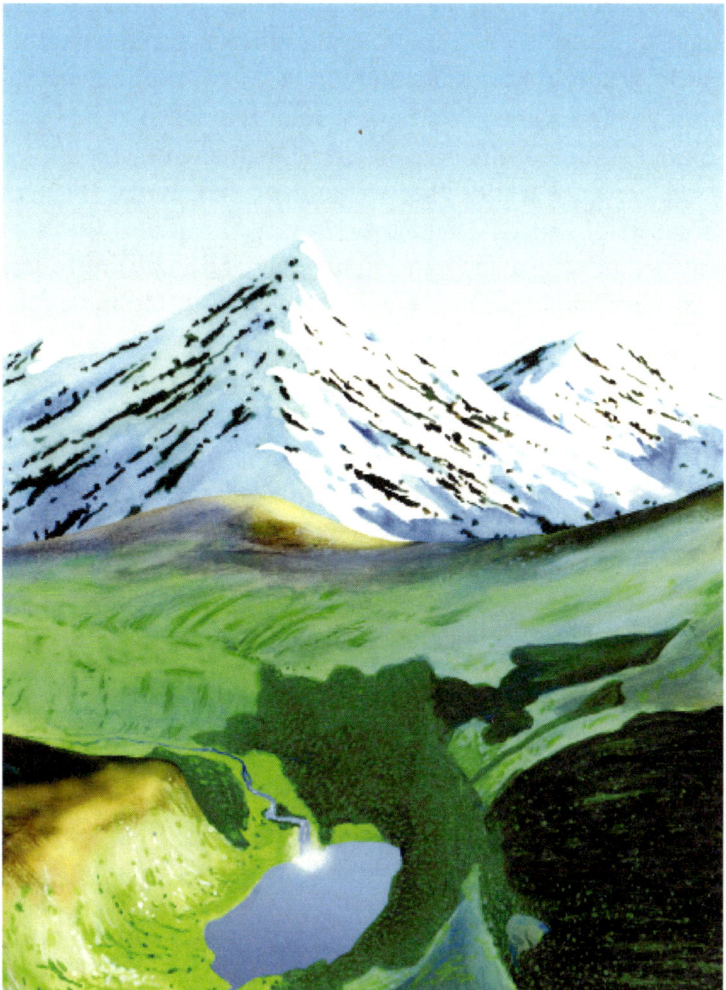

The very act of agreeing to come together in an alliance would in itself be extraordinarily beneficial. In such a beautiful and peaceful place men of different faiths could meet in friendship to study or reflect. Each religion could construct simple accommodations for their needs – nothing brash, nothing ostentatious. Places of worship, too, might be built, but none more conspicuous or grand than any other.

On walking trails which would be developed through some sections of this wilderness reserve people of different faiths would stop awhile and sit together and share food and a joke. They might discuss elements of their differing beliefs. In so doing they will become less strange to each other and more clearly recognize the sameness of all men in their quest for the One Who Is Beyond All Comprehension. Surely such a prize would be an enormous gain for all religions? And no religion would be compromised in its beliefs.

The first reaction to such a proposal would probably be that it is impossible to implement, that too many barriers would stand in the way. With anything that is difficult a dozen well-meaning men will step forward and deem that it cannot be done. A thing may be difficult, but that does not make it impossible! People of vision swept aside the nay sayers and put men on the moon. Surely religious men of vision could accomplish what is being asked here? It would only take a few good people from the great religions to come together and say: "Let us do it. Let us join in this great adventure together." For this alone it is surely worth putting courage on the line: to reach out to each other and to participate together in this wonderful undertaking. The gain in mutual understanding would be enormous.

Islamic, Christian, Sikh, Buddhist, Jewish and Hindu leaders might agree to confer together to create between them the first 'World Religious Nature Reserve'. And such a protected area – protected in law in the manner that applies to all great national parks and reserves – would keep from harm the myriad forms of life within its boundaries. What is now needed is for enlightened men and women of the great religions of the world to discuss together what is proposed here.

1. *See* Reg Morrison and Helen Grasswill: *Australia: A Timeless Grandeur*, Lansdowne Press, Sydney, 1981, p.13, cols.1-2.

On Poverty and the Protection of Species

I will kill the last parrot on Earth

> *In southeast Asia, Africa and South America deforestation is occurring at a rapid rate and at each review more tropical rainforest birds are classified as threatened.*[1]

For a time laws and wildlife rangers may protect nature reserves – but only for a time. If people do not support what is being done on their behalf then these methods will end in failure.

This is particularly true in poor countries where millions of people depend on wild lands for what such lands can yield in food, medicines, grazing, and fuel wood for their fires. They will also trap birds and butterflies and reptiles and mammals for what they can get by selling these into the live-animal trade. And they will stand against all laws to do so, for they will do what is necessary that they may feed their children. They will take from coral reefs fish for food and sell to tourists dried seahorses out of sweet-jars. They will sell pipefish and shells and sponges – and if need be the very coral itself. And make no mistake, we too would do the same in their circumstances, and no law would stand in our way, for we will feed our children. Poverty can do that.

With this reality staring us in the face, the management of

such wild areas needs to include within its responsibilities the accommodation of local people. No conservation programme will succeed in the long term if it excludes people who need what the forest can give for their survival. Hard-nosed conservationists must accept this reality. There must be engagement with local people in how an area is to be managed if both people and wildlife are to survive. How do we stop poor people from killing the one remaining parrot in a rainforest? Remove their poverty.

It is an easy matter to sit in relative comfort and talk of wildlife conservation. It is another reality to attempt to feed a family for a week on less than what a rich woman might throw away after one meal. A billion people live on less than $1.25 a day. At this level of poverty concern for wildlife does not register even a single blip on the radar. Without a thought I will kill any animal that my children may eat. I will pluck the very sparrows from the air. I will shoot the last crane in China if need be. I will trap hen harriers and harvest their eggs and take the money on offer that my children may eat. I will kill the last deer in the forest. I will take the skin and meat and bones and the very whiskers of Indian tigers that my family may survive. I will take the eggs of turtles, I will take their flesh; I will take the tusks of elephants and their meat too. I will shoot rhino for the magic in their horns. I will drop bears into pit-traps and continue to do so to feed my children. And if there is but a single bear remaining I will set my trap one more time. I will cut down trees in nature reserves. I will take fuel wood from the slopes of mountains and not care that the hills slide down in gullies and avalanches, for I will have fuel to cook the little I can find. At this level of poverty you can kill some of us with your police and soldiers and your park rangers – but we will continue to do these things. Yes, wildlife will lose, and there will be no discussion amongst us that it should be otherwise, for we will feed our children.

Stark this may be, but it has the energy of honesty about it; and if we are serious about conservation, we need, as a world people, to confront the despair of the poor – our poor. More to the point, we need a solution – for humanity's sake – so that people are not left in such conditions. This is not a problem that conservationists can solve. It is wildly outside their experience, but it is a massive social failure which directly threatens the survival of thousands of plant and animal species. It is a failure that threatens wildlife habitats on an enormous front.

Because of their desperation and attempt to improve a little on their circumstances, impoverished people filter into areas that are designated national parks or nature reserves. They trickle into back valleys or ever higher up mountains and further out into swamplands to take what they can find there. They compete directly with the wildlife that lives in these areas – often the last places for such wildlife to go. Here the poverty of people and the conservation of species confront each other in a terrible struggle. Such poverty is a disgrace and it demeans all of us; but we will confront mountainous difficulties in attempting to deal with it.

Some might complain that these people should do something to take themselves out of their situation. But people at this level of defeat lack the energy and the mental agility to fight the distress that engulfs them every which way they turn. They need direct intervention from the rest of us. In face of such appalling deprivation, talk of habitat protection must fall silent. This poverty is real and it is hard and it must be confronted. It is easy to say that, but in a practical sense where do we go from this statement?

The first difficulty we need to come to terms with is that the problem is complex. It will not be solved easily. It will not be solved quickly or without the expenditure of enormous resources. It will not be solved in the absence of a worldwide structured approach to defeat it. The scale is daunting. To date we have thrown billions of dollars against it, yet poverty continues to defy us. It has remorselessly sucked at resources with little to show for what was spent. Clearly it is time to review our poverty programmes. We need to approach the problem as we would a war. War kills people, so does poverty. We cannot hope to succeed simultaneously on all fronts. Better to take one country, or one region, at a time and focus our resources there until the problem is truly eliminated. Just one such success would give spurs to our confidence that we can indeed defeat global poverty. Countries so helped would in turn be expected to contribute towards killing poverty in other parts of the world.

We need to make a distinction between famine and poverty. Each can readily seesaw back and forth into the camp of the other. Each kills, but famine hits the red light and screams urgency. Famines can be catastrophic and engulf whole regions. In my own country – from 1845 to 1847 – we had a catastrophic famine. Whole families were found dead with the stain of grass on their lips. There is one account of a man carrying his dying child on his back for twelve miles to the house of a rich person. He was turned away at the door. He returned the following day and was rejected once more. On the third day when he came to the house to plead once again for food it was too late. The child he had been carrying had died during the journey. At that time my own people lived on a dirt farm. They had a small field of beans. A young girl was found dead in the field. She had been eating raw beans. That field is now referred to as 'the bean field'. During those grim years the roll-call of the dead relentlessly grew. People fled to America and Canada. If you visit Boston, Massachusetts, you will see sandwiched between the Old South Meeting House and the Border Bookstore on Washington Street a memorial to the Irish famine victims of that time. It proclaims that in 1847 alone, thirty-seven thousand Irish refugees landed in Boston. In the same year the good people of Massachusetts sent eight hundred tons of food and clothing to Ireland to help relieve some of the suffering. Today Ireland is relatively prosperous. But whether it is Russia or China or Africa or South America, famine is still a reality. Intermittently we are galvanised into doing something, and we move impressive tons of food and medicines against it. Our sporadic surges of contributing through famine relief schemes drive the disturbing images from our television screens; and when the famine gathers up the last of its allotted children and drags them down into the soil, we settle again for poverty.

But poverty is famine by the slow road. We don't die spectacularly, but we die. We die, too, of disease that would not kill us if we had enough to eat. We die unrecorded without TV images.

Governments and international agencies, and – bless their generous natures – countless voluntary bodies, commit themselves to ridding the world of poverty. But poverty persists, and it shows no signs of abating. In this respect, what is offered here in these few words is set down in bluntness and with affection for our global humanity – and in full recognition of the deficiencies that lie in all of us. It is offered not in order to insult any individual or organisation or institution; it is offered simply as how things are, as distinct from how we might wish them to be.

It is estimated that thirty-five million people die each year from starvation. We are appalled to read of the death of ten people killed in a bus crash, or of fifty people who plunged to their deaths when a block of flats collapsed, or of a hundred times that figure killed in an earthquake. But where is our disturbed conscience in face of such numbers dying from starvation?

Brute lack of resources, which makes it impossible for a family to put food on the table, is the underlying cause of poverty. The reasons for this are varied, complex and – for the most part – man-made. Poverty, in many situations, is the twin brother of war or the sister of populations out of control. Projections regarding the growth of human populations have appeared in many reports. It is sufficient to say that, however we do it, we need to bring our population into equilibrium with what this planet can sustain. Beyond that point we can produce more of our kind, but we do so at the expense of other species. We need to be clear about this – and it is the poorer countries that are showing the greatest increase in human numbers.

How are such countries to reduce their numbers? There are hard social and religious pressures stacked against effective solutions. Where infant mortality is consistently high, large families are a crude insurance that some children will survive into adulthood. Also, within many communities, having large families bestows social status. This does not only apply to the women; being *macho* is characteristic of some cultures – it defines a man. We should not underestimate the pressure on males in such societies to prove their ability to father children. However we are going to go about it, we must confront this need to limit our population.

There are other factors too that are undermining our ability to fight poverty. The uncertainty of weather patterns in recent years adds to the difficulty. Families living in desert areas can quickly find themselves in a famine because of the fickleness of the weather. Indeed, is there ever a point when we finally concede that certain lands are now no longer habitable and that, as such, no additional moneys should be spent on them? If we admit to this, are we saying that people should be moved off those lands? – and if so, where are they to go? Alternatively, do we try to sustain these families indefinitely on land which, for all practical purposes, has become desert and cannot support their food needs? Water pumps and better quality seed may help some, but such assistance will be of no benefit to those without adequate land.

These people need to be offered an alternative means of making a living; most, however, will be unskilled for such work and will be illiterate.

Rudimentary training will be a need. Such jobs that result are likely to be menial and badly paid, but they would be the first step out of the relentless suck and pull of poverty for many people. Where the ownership of a cup and plate registers as wealth, these jobs would be welcome. Also, such employment, however lowly, would give structure, stability and hope to lives that had had none until then. Workers at the beginning of this process may never experience riches but some of their children may achieve comfort, and a number of their grandchildren may become wealthy. We have to be realists in all of this. We are faced with the need to create millions of jobs in highly disadvantaged countries.

What would entice multinational companies to build factories in these places? Profit – and political stability. Multinational companies are in the business of risk assessment. Why would they want to set up factories where nothing but disadvantage stares them in the face? They wouldn't – unless they see the prospect of profit.

With financial inducements these companies can be encouraged to sniff the wind and see potential in what they find there. We must be clear in our thinking here – profit motives drive these companies. They must be given space to make profit. Inducements to tip the balance in that direction should be made available through the UN.

In many poor regions there is a common occurrence that curtails the giving by rich countries. This is the practice of corruption. Corruption occurs in all countries but in some of the poorer ones it is endemic. It can happen at every level, from heads of state down through layers of officials who are only moved to make things happen if a bribe is on offer. Many multinational companies know the rules of embracing the bribe system if business is to be done in these places.

Professional bribe-fixers can be hired to smooth the way to win contracts or sell products.

And why should we be shocked by this? Uncertainty of employment can be an ever-present reality in these countries. The job I have today might be taken from me tomorrow for no other reason than that a minister's son or a minister's cousin or his wife's brother wants the position. I am fearful therefore. I do not know when a telephone call will come through that will change all. 'Get it while you can' sets up residence in one more brain, and the bribe culture grows by an additional person: "You want something done today, sir? I regret that that is impossible ... Oh, five dollars! Thank you, sir. I'll see what I can do." Such can be the normality of business in some countries. Bribery at the highest level of government, where the real power resides, can run into millions of dollars. This is money for an enviable lifestyle. This is corruption in the heavy meaning of the term.

Poverty destroys so much that could be good in the world. It diminishes happiness and threatens peace; it destabilizes governments; it festers ethnic animosities; it bolsters religious prejudices – powerful enough reasons to compel all of us to reflect on the need for a solution to world poverty.

There are hundreds of charitable organisations that have for so long attempted to do the impossible with minimal resources at their disposal. These brave people often put themselves in personal danger in order to bring comfort to the poor and do this grinding work with little thanks from the rest of us.

The only organisation we have that is of sufficient size and carries enough authority to confront poverty at a world level is the United Nations; and it will need the support of the citizens of the world if it is to succeed in ripping even a single country out of the clawing hands of deep poverty. But for such support the United Nations needs to periodically reinvigorate itself. It needs to revisit and revitalize its anti-poverty programmes. The UN holds the elimination of poverty as one of its stated priorities, but most people are unaware of even a small percentage of the work the United Nations does in this respect. This is a failure of communication on a massive scale.

The UN needs therefore to make itself, and the work it does, far more visible to all of us on our television channels. Indeed, it should have its *own* channel to show us its success stories. It should show us where it has failed, too, and why these programmes failed. In this way it would motivate citizens to engage with their governments to become more involved with the UN programmes in this worldwide project to eliminate poverty. The UN, as a consequence, would be viewed by citizens as a more sympathetic and better understood organisation. Its authority would increase.

The United Nations is, however, encrusted with complicated procedures. Sectional interests circumscribe it on all sides. It is riveted through with petty jealousies. Some member states are not as upright and open as they should be. The UN is simply a reflection of all of us writ large; but for all that, it is all we have.

It has to be recognized here that to hold co-operation among nations this organization must walk a very thin line indeed. Diplomacy must be fiendishly difficult at this level; but is there really a need for bureaucracy to operate at all levels down the chain of command?

There should be but a single UN programme to eliminate poverty, with one Chief Executive Officer in charge to run this business – as a business. There should be an independent group, answerable only to this CEO, to evaluate the success of each project on its completion. The CEO should have the authority to take appropriate steps when things do not go as intended. Staff not sufficiently motivated should be replaced. The CEO must be given the authority to do this.

The United Nations has a great achievement against its

name for which it should accept our admiration – the elimination of smallpox. By any standard this is a magnificent success story for the World Health Organization. Indeed, I do not believe that the world's people have ever given enough acknowledgement to the UN for what it has accomplished here. This organization should take courage from this success when focusing anew on the even more complex goal of poverty elimination.

Given the scale of poverty that confronts it, even the UN cannot hope to conquer it in one global bite. It must break the problem into smaller regions and focus its resources on one or two regions at a time, until poverty is removed from these areas. For this to happen scarce resources will have to be temporarily held back from some countries. Hard choices these, but attempting to do for all in one go hasn't worked. Something else needs to be tried.

The UN needs to insist on even tougher demands when dealing with rich nations to fund this programme. It should call upon the people of the world for their support through a worldwide publicity campaign, targeted not at governments but at citizens.

Harsher rules must come, too, with all funding to countries in need. Some conditions might be unpalatable to many recipient countries, but they will need to be agreed to if a poverty elimination package is to be offered. If government leaders find that they cannot accept the harsh conditions, then, without hesitation, the aid on offer should be moved elsewhere. This should be done firmly and without rancour. Poverty elimination is too important an issue for leniency to prevail. Resources will be too precious to squander on governments who will not conform to what is expected of them if an acceptable standard of living is to be achieved.

Corruption must be eliminated within poverty aid projects. If those in power insist on "a little something" for their co-operation, the programme should immediately be withdrawn and the reasons why made widely known. We owe this to the donor countries. So important is this issue that not only should costs for all projects be approved by UN personnel but all payments should be made directly by them without placing *any* parts of the budgets into the hands of recipient countries.

The curtailment of a country's population growth might be a condition for access to aid, even though this subject is a minefield. This stipulation may prove enormously difficult for some countries, but hard choices will need to be made if poverty is to be eradicated. And where dictators are in power it will take fine skills and fine judgements by UN officials to decide whether or not to engage with these regimes for the good of their people, and under what circumstances.

Will any of this succeed? It will not succeed unless far larger amounts of resources are placed at the disposal of the UN. Eliminating poverty is a moral imperative. It is also a wildlife conservation issue.

1. Richard Mackay: *The Atlas of Endangered Species*, Earthscan Publications Ltd, London, 2002, p. 76.

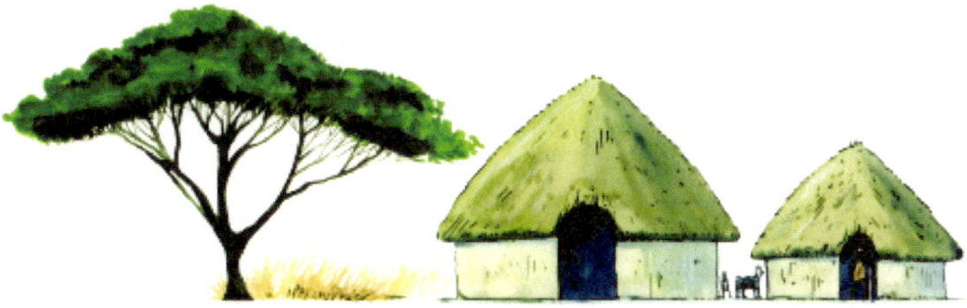

> **What the super-rich can do to protect species**

The Hundred-Million-Dollar Club

Business and Nature

Enormous resources will be needed to cripple poverty. Funding will be needed beyond what governments will pledge to the UN. Where might some of this additional money come from?

The super-wealthy might be persuaded here. Some have unimaginable disposable riches, far beyond what most of us can even visualize. So the question might be asked: how much does anyone really need to be happy? The fabulously rich cannot be coerced into giving up part of their wealth, no matter how good the cause. They cannot be coerced, but they might be persuaded.

Let's put down a marker here. Most people would like lots of money for the things it can buy for themselves and for their families. But how much does any one person really need? There has to be an upper limit beyond which there is no further return on personal contentment. If that is so, why does anyone need money beyond this limit?

The drive for private wealth can surpass what is needed for a comfortable life. It can spiral ever upwards into an endless and pointless journey of personal acquisition. This chasing of wealth beyond any sensible need may have something to do with satisfying the ego. We may not be able to define with ease what ego is, but by heavens it is there in all of us, and in some more powerfully than in others. Nietzsche saw the 'will to power' everywhere, even in the asceticism of great saints and in the resentment of condemnatory moralists.

Pecking order, it seems, is not just confined to chickens! *I am better than you. I hold higher status in society. What I do is more important than what you do.* We should never underestimate the intensity packing in behind these views of ourselves. In this world of competition you own twelve factories and I a mere eleven; at social gatherings the difference is noted. I am driven to do better. At last – four more factories. Who is now king of the hill? Who's the daddy? Reason enough now to be seen swinging a seven iron at the Country Club – until a newcomer announces the dreaded words – 'Sixteen factories'.

We are capable of killing because of ego; and where two equally powerful egos clash – well, rational thought steps out of the way. We are then in Napoleonic territory. But all of us, not just the big hitters, need to acknowledge our egotistical natures and that our struggle for money and power can sometimes sweep us beyond what is sensible.

In saying this, I am not denigrating competition or the striving to outdo others. Millions of jobs depend on the risktakers who drive our industries. It is simply a recognition of the fact that all of us, in our own particular way, are driven by egos that demand attention. Many of these people genuinely enjoy what they do and the fabulous wealth that it brings. Indeed, given a choice these lucky people could not conceive of any other lifestyle. Others simply enjoy the fire of competition. Some feel a true responsibility for their employees and the families of their employees. For reasons that are less clear, some heads of industries are workaholics, identifying themselves entirely with what they do, and in this enclosed world they find their own brand of contentment.

This brings me back again to the question of how much is enough for a person to be truly happy. So many of us have so much 'stuff' now that we have little time to enjoy it. At every turn we are encouraged to buy the 'new' because it is bigger – better – faster – than the previous acquisition. We believe we are buying power when all we are purchasing is a product. We trade our contentment in the silence of being for gadgets. It might be said that we have become hollow people with a desperate need to fill the void in our lives with 'things', in order to regain what we have put aside. So where might we go from here?

We might, for the moment, dissociate wealth from the work that generates that wealth. Does anyone need more than say $100,000,000 to be truly content? Surely anything beyond that stupendous amount would not increase a person's sense of contentment! I suspect that in most people's minds a hundred million would do just fine – would do way more than just fine! I am not suggesting that contentment rests solely on being wealthy. But wealth does play its part and we are attempting here to set an upper limit on what that figure should be.

One hundred million would buy a fine lifestyle indeed, with more than enough laid aside for contingency situations should they arise. Yes, for the great majority of us a figure far below $100,000,000 would do just fine. But if we agree that a hundred million dollars is tops for contentment and anything above it is meaningless, then, when we contrast the lifestyle of somebody who is immensely wealthy with that of a poor person who has to push bits of rubbish into a flame in order to boil water in a tin can, we begin to think of towering wealth as being something rather shoddy.

This is not to demean extremely well-heeled people. Far

from it. Most of us have been brought up with the ambition to accumulate what we can. Given the opportunity, who would not try to achieve great wealth? But accumulating riches can quickly become an end in itself, a badge of achievement, the money itself of no consequence.

When is enough, truly enough? We have never worked out the level, even in the broadest of terms, of what is sufficient. If we could do that, then on reaching that amount we would feel that society too could acknowledge our achievements. This level of 'enough' might be pitched quite high. It might be set at a level where to reach it one would need to be very rich indeed. But need this bar be set at infinity?

We have established that the endless accumulation of things for their own sake could threaten one's potential to be happy. We might agree on that point – but the ever-present ego, like a wasp in a jar, can drive us beyond the barrier of good sense. So how do we assuage our egos?

Well, we might agree on what we could refer to as *the bar of personal contentment*. This would be the level of wealth at which a person could live in luxury for all of his or her life. Let's say we set this bar at $100,000,000 – an unattainable figure for just about all of us, but nevertheless for the super-rich a goal that can easily be surpassed. At such a level of success the rich person might conclude that he or she had now got more money than would ever be needed and that to strive for more would be pointless.

Having thus reached their *bar of personal contentment*, these people might consider a proposition that would add enormously to their sense of self-worth: that all accumulated wealth beyond that point should be streamed into a fund for the elimination of poverty. By participating in such a wonderful undertaking the super-rich could still continue competing as fiercely as they had ever done with each other, if this is still their desire, except that now their surplus wealth would be working towards a different end, an aim that would give them deep personal satisfaction and wide social acclaim: collectively they would be making millions to help the poor. And we already have a precedent for this sea change in thinking.

We might reflect a moment on the extraordinary generosity of three men – Warren Buffett, Chuck Feeney and Bill Gates. All three have accumulated immense fortunes and are putting billions of dollars into programmes aimed at fighting poverty. And the interesting thing is that all three men seem to be just plum happy with their lives. They do not seem in any doubt that what they are doing is anything other than the right thing. These men, and other individuals too, are setting a trend that more members of the super-rich class might want to follow.

Suppose we could put in place something that we would call *The Hundred-Million-Dollar Club*, or some other agreed denomination of wealth. To be part of this select club men and women would promise that their own personal wealth would not rise above that figure, and that they would indeed channel any wealth accumulated above that level into a fund to eliminate poverty. This fund, in turn, would be managed by hard-nosed business men and women and run as a business with 'value for money' as its goal. They would take no prisoners in face of corruption or nepotism in potential recipient countries seeking aid.

If such a programme were to be put in place it would help the world's poor and would help protect species where the poor are in conflict with wildlife over the possession of habitats. Belonging to such an altruistic club would set its members apart in the eyes of the world. An annual report, forwarded to each member, would show what had been achieved on their behalf. This would give satisfaction far beyond that which could be achieved by the mere acquisition of 'things'. Members of this club could truly say "I am part of something great and good in the world."

The Hundred-Million-Dollar Club would release billions of dollars into poverty aid programmes. The super-rich might like to debate this, and agree among themselves to set up a structure that equates to *The Hundred-Million-Dollar Club*. The poor need your help, and wildlife and plants would benefit too.

A World Dance Day for Nature

Dance, children, for all that is music!

Let us pick a day. On that day let the children of the world dance together under the sun. Let them dance in their own countries but let them know that other children are dancing too. Let them know that English children, Japanese children, German children, children in Amsterdam, South African children, the children of Burma and the children of Adelaide are dancing. Let them know that American children in San Francisco and Amarillo and around the Little Belt Mountains are all a-dance.

Let them know that they are dancing for the joy of being children; that they are dancing for the sheer delight in existence; that they are dancing in celebration of nature in all her wonder; that they are dancing for the joy of the dance. And, in the movement of all of that rhythm, let us celebrate the majesty of life itself; and perhaps we, reserved adults that we are, might be infected by the happiness of our children or our grandchildren and dance a little too.

In our simple dance we should not dance for us alone. We should dance for the starfish. We should dance for the snow worms. We should dance for the musk turtles. We should dance for the snake flies. We should dance for the silence of the great whales. We should dance for the symmetry of the tuna. We should dance for the beauty of sea hares. We should dance for the snipefish and the magpie larks. We should dance for the stalactites in the Cango Caves; we should dance for the stromatolites in the warm Australian seas. We should dance for the ice fields of Antarctica. And finally we should dance for our planet sweeping through the silence of space.

We should dance, too, a requiem. A requiem for all the species that tried and failed. We should dance for the great auk; we should dance for the Japanese wolf and for the Labrador duck; we should dance for the elephant birds and the Portuguese ibex; we should dance for the quagga and the giant Irish deer.

We should dance for the life that will follow us; for the joy that that life will have in its moment of existence. And when the dancing stops we should cheer with the joy of knowing that for the first time all the people of the planet danced together and that things will never be the same again. Such a day will be worthy of remembrance!

The land of the Bisnois[1]
India

The Great Indian Desert that lies away to the west of the city of Delhi is a formidable place. Yet in this harsh landscape there is an area rich in vegetation and birds and animals. It is a place owned by a strong people.

Five hundred years ago this part of India suffered invasion and famine. Forests were cut down, animals killed. The land became barren. Guru Jameshwarji observed these things and concluded that forests must be planted and cherished if the land was to be restored. His followers listened to what the wise man had to say. In time, where there had been no trees, forests grew. They grew because the Bisnois tended their trees. The trees cast shade that cooled the hot ground. They shed leaves that enriched the impoverished soil. In the presence of the thickening forests the land grew fertile again.

Then, if legends are to be believed, a terrible thing happened. Almost three centuries ago a huge and ancient fort at Jodhpur fell into disrepair. Large amounts of trees were needed if the great fort was to be restored. Where would such trees come from? Only the lands of the Bisnois, in all of that broad desert, had trees in any numbers.

Men were sent out to search for suitable trees. The Bisnois would not agree that their trees should be cut. But the men had their instructions. The Bisnois protested in every way that they could, but their trees were felled to repair the great fort. To demonstrate the depth of respect in which they held their forests, something more was needed. What could they do to convince the Maharaja, who had ordered the repairs to the fort, of the degree of their concern for their trees?

There was only one further thing that they could do. Many of the people killed themselves. (Other sources say that they embraced their trees to protect them and were killed so that the trees could be cut down.) When the Maharaja was brought word of what was happening he was shocked and ordered that no more trees be felled.

Today large numbers of trees grow on Bisnois land, while all around the desert is barren. Wild animals and birds live among these trees. The Bisnois have a lot to teach us.

1. *See* Kailash Sankhala: 'Prospering from the Desert' in *The Law of the Mother – Protecting Indigenous People in Protected Areas*, ed. Elizabeth Kemf, Sierra Club Books, San Francisco, 1993, pp. 18-22.

Dream of a world you would like
Résumé

We have problems in our relationship to wildlife. If we are to have any chance of making things better, change must happen within each one of us. We must begin to value nature. We must value her simply for her own sake. We can no longer depend on rules and laws alone to protect her. Left to themselves rules and laws will fail us. A change in our thinking is what is needed. As things stand we are engaged in deception. We deceive ourselves that we are protecting nature. We are not. If we don't protect her, species will continue to become extinct. It is no more complicated than that. The alternative is to carry on as we have and to accept modern extinctions as inevitable and man-made. If we decide not to do anything and to accept the consequences, then this will at least have the dignity of honesty about it.

If, however, we make the decision that change is needed, then that degree of change should not fall short of what is required. It should not simply be that we donate more bits of land here and there to nature as though that were enough. It isn't. We need more clearly to see nature for what she brings into our lives. If we succeed in this we will discover that she can be like an old friend, continually delighting us with the surprises she throws our way. In this light we should accept her not just for the grand statements of a mountainside ablaze with alpine flowers or for her display of a million salmon on the move or the drumming of the hooves of 100,000 wildebeest; we should accept her too in the small, in the rustle of a mouse in a hedgerow, in what it is to be a mouse. We should accept her in the precise placing of a foot by a water rail. We should accept her in the beauty of a fine snail moving about after rain. In these things we can find contentment in being part of the multiplicity of life on this Earth.

Planet Dancing has struggled to engage us in practical ways to find our road back towards nature. The giving of 'nature names' to our children is a practical step along this road. Nature naming does not need an organisation in place for it to happen. We simply bestow these names on our young. What is needed here is the determination of parents to engage with this idea, for their children's sake and for the benefit of wildlife. Nature naming is a simple idea yet its effects could be profound. But to succeed we need parents to do this now.

There will always be cynics who will say that such a simple thing as this is not practical. Their contempt must be borne in silence. We might ask them what *their* practical solutions are to the problems that are driving species to extinction. This practice of giving nature names to our children can be the first flickering of a world conservation movement in which we can all participate. It is entirely understandable that at the beginning of this process some will feel a bit foolish about giving their children such names. That they will still do it will be to their credit. And if people persevere in giving names from nature to their children, it will in time become a most natural thing to do. In all of this we need to keep our minds focused on what it is that we are working to achieve. We are attempting to change society's conduct and attitude towards wildlife.

Life is to be lived. The *Children-of-the-World Nature Reserve* project would be a fun event. Thousands of adults across many countries would be needed to organise this. Parents could explain to their children what is being attempted here. Then they should leave it to their children to decide to donate a little of their savings to the project – or not to donate. If this idea is to succeed as intended, there must be no coercion to donate. The important thing here is that the child thinks about the issue.

The idea of such a reserve, created by donations from children, is certainly new. Its real value though will not be in the formation of one more nature reserve but in the change it will bring about in the minds of the children who had to make the choice. To those children nature will no longer be a fuzzy issue. It will become real, and it will need nurturing if it is to be saved.

It will take enthusiasm and excitement to bring such a reserve into existence. It will take the skills of a committee to blueprint the way. This committee, in turn, will need seed funding to explore the best line of approach. Not one coin from any child should be spent on anything other than the purchase, or leasing, and the running of the reserve itself. Seed funding will therefore need to come from some other source. A wealthy individual, or individuals who in the past have been touched by the magnificence of nature, might want to consider this.

Such a special reserve, created by the donations of millions of children, will be a wonderful achievement in its own right. Children in many lands will go to bed at night knowing that somewhere in the world there is a special place where wildlife is protected and that they are part of what makes it possible. This will imprint on children the beginning of a conservation ethic. This ethic will grow with them into their adult lives. As adults they will make political and business decisions, and these decisions will be made with the value of nature built into their thinking. This will be conservation ethics operating in a practical way.

Probably the most difficult idea raised in *Planet Dancing* is the prospect of creating a *World Religious Wilderness Reserve* under the collective ownership of the great religions of the world. Yet, when we think about it, it should be the easiest of all the projects. What makes it difficult – although it should be added not impossible – are the strongly held views of the important religious groups and their difficulties in reaching common ground with each other. No religion should be criticized for this. Such intransigence is simply a reflection of us all. Against that, a religious wilderness reserve should be seen to be non-threatening and non-contentious. Indeed, if religions would agree to come together for the creation of such a reserve, it might enable them, in time, to meet again on more weighty matters.

World conservation organisations might wish to discuss this idea and agree a structure on how such a reserve might best be brought about for the benefit of the wildlife it might contain. Religious leaders would need help with this part of the proposal. Conservationists might arrange a symposium to which representatives of the world's major religions would be invited. The proposal for such a reserve could be presented as a subsection of a conference arranged to address the subject of 'Nature and Religion in the Modern World'. Conservation bodies might issue a call for papers to be presented on these themes.

Some years ago I visited Topkapi Palace in Istanbul in Turkey. In this palace there was a fine display case brightly illuminated. It had but one object on display, a large diamond suspended by a thread which gave the illusion that the precious stone was floating in the air. A tiny light, skilfully placed, made the beautiful gem sparkle, as a fine stone should. Beside this display case a soldier stood at attention. The diamond clearly belonged to the world of 'great worth'. This stone of 86 carats, reputed to have been found in a dump in the seventeenth century, was traded back then, it is alleged, for three spoons and is now referred to as the 'Spoonmaker's Diamond.'

When I approached the case the soldier suddenly dropped out of his military pose and gestured with the tips of his fingers that I should draw closer, the better to see the diamond.

The man was ecstatic that a foreign visitor was taking such an interest in this magnificent jewel. He talked excitedly, repeatedly waving his arms and pointing at the display case. That I did not understand a word he was saying was not important. His whole attitude, his every gesture, spoke of the pride he felt in such a great treasure. Indeed I have no doubt that if I had attempted to steal the Spoonmaker's Diamond he would have shot me dead – with several bullets to register the enormity of my crime.

I am sure that security men and women in other countries would act in no less a manner to protect their great treasures. In my own country we have many magnificent and intricately worked manuscripts dating back a thousand years or more. We too would make sure that they wouldn't get damaged. They are part of our heritage; they represent us and help define us as a people. If they were destroyed or stolen we would feel diminished. Sometimes it is difficult to rationalize such feelings but if necessary we would even be prepared to die rather than lose our heritage.

So the question needs to be asked: should we not protect our wildlife heritage with the same forcefulness with which we protect precious stones? Is not the culmination of millions of years of evolution as worthy of protection? Should wildlife not be protected from extinction by as great a weight of law as that which protects great paintings or a Louis XVI secrétaire or a Ming wine jar? It is interesting to speculate on our fine Turkish soldier once more. He may well go hunting at weekends and without a thought take a rare saker falcon out of the Turkish sky.

If we are to have a hope of protecting species we need to see wildlife as treasure. We need to see habitat as no less important than art. Are not the great tigers and the great rhino of the world as precious as the art in the Vatican? Should they not be defended from harm with the same vigour we defend the works of Vermeer? How should we treat those hunters who kill or take orang-utans – precious creatures that belong to the entire world? How should we treat those who destroy the forests where these magnificent animals live? How should we treat those who shoot the poetry of cranes or the dignity of condors – birds whose splendour can bring a lump to our throats?

Species under threat, whether they be mountain gorillas or mahogany trees or macaws, must become the concern of us all. Laws and regulations in the end will not protect species. They will only be protected by the majority of us wanting it to be so. If we do not discard our present duplicity towards conservation, then species will continue to become extinct.

We need to be clear about this: if we continue sleepwalking past what is occurring, then extinctions will increase. We will attempt to shield ourselves from guilt. We will claim it was unavoidable. We will talk of how we did our best to protect these things, but we will know it to be a lie. Can we not store the blueprints of vanishing species in gene banks? Surely there is hope in that? In the distant future, when things become better, will we not be able to recreate species from frozen tissue? Even if we could do that, where will the habitats be for these things to live and grow as they should?

Maybe all of this draining away of species into extinction is inevitable. Maybe the millions of 'tryers' are simply part of one super-process in nature, the supreme weeding out of the many who cannot exist under the dominance of the few. Maybe all of these tryers, in spite of their beauty, their majestic movements and wonderful dance, never really had a chance.

One species has finally emerged out of sustained competition as dominant. Maybe it is part of this process that thousands of others now drop away into the deep fade and finally into oblivion. Their consolation might be that they have played a part in a wonderful process that could only conclude in the emergence of one winner, all creatures, all evolution culminating in the primacy of the one. This dominant species, in its wisdom and for its own purposes, will more forcefully select which lines of 'tryers' it will allow to continue. Oh, it will not admit the word 'allow', but it is in fact part of what is occurring. The great tribe of grasses will rank high on the retention list. So, too, will some of the timber trees and important root crops and medicinal plants and some fish and herbivores as well. But what will be the standing of hawks and owls and parakeets and coral reefs? Who will speak for wolves? Who will speak for anteaters and honey possum? In this new world will there be a place for zebras? Will filefish have a value, or lacewings or bobwhites? Where are our beautiful tigers to go? Where might we see dormice or white-tailed eagles or pygmy sunbirds?

We have reached the stage in our development when we must debate these questions. If we don't, then things will continue to slip away. They will go without fanfare and even without our awareness of their passing. And still we will continue to ease our guilt by claiming that *nothing could have been done.*

No doubt some lines will continue in spite of us. They will survive, because they will take what they can find and continue. In this new world there will be far fewer species to delight us, far fewer things to inspire us, far fewer things to compel us to wonder at it all. Maybe that too is inevitable. Maybe we will go to other worlds and find there things to replace, after a fashion, what we have lost on our own planet. There will be no more snow geese or white ibis or buzzards. They will have long gone into holograms and sound recordings. And at such a time we too will have moved on in our evolution and become star people. Perhaps that is indeed our future.

For now, though, we don't seem willing that any species should slip away into extinction, but *we* are the cause of it happening. We still wish it were otherwise. There is hope even in that. There is a feeling in the air that it is not right that such things should occur. This may not yet be a strong feeling, but that it is there at all gives grounds for hope. Maybe we recognize in some unclear way that all of us, humans and other species, have come an unbelievably long way together.

Maybe we will recognize that we were all companions on a very long journey, that we are all old friends who may have had their differences on occasion, but for all that are still friends. Against the smothering blanket of time there is some comfort in having so many friends about one.

When we finally go to the stars, we may discover that the old friends we left behind on Earth are all that we have. Maybe then our eyes might be opened to see finally the value of these things. Maybe then we might discover that all our histories originated from the same speck of animation, that all the old friends are cousins after all. There is hope for conservation in that.

THE END

ADDENDUM

Poets dreaming

Poets are the dreamwalkers who walk through the superficial and spin the magic of what is there unseen. Yet, can the organizing of world events for nature ever be more than dreams? Two poets considered the proposition.

"We've settled for dreams in the past. There was a bit of comfort in that."

"Yes, but just for once, could there be more than that?"

"It would take many to organise such events."

"Well, what if there were many? That way it would be easier."

"There would need to be thousands."

"Right then! Let there be thousands."

The two friends looked at each other, each man's eyes shining with the possibilities, each fighting against the possibility of it being just one more dream. But this time it could be different, the feel was different. People wanted now to be part of something indefinable, something that would make a difference.

"So what would you do if you were given a free hand?"

"A completely free hand?"

"Got it."

"Then I would pick the year 2020. In that year I would ask the people of the world to come together to plan a number of spectacular events to celebrate all life."

"That would be a great thing to do."

The poets looked at each other – and smiled.